·THE BAY·

ISLANDS

WHAUWHAU BEACH

CLIFFS

SHACK

WHALERS BEACH

LOST BAY

BACH

FISH HOSPITAL

MRS CROSS'S

THE WHISTLERS

ACH REEK

JUMPING PIT

FORT

MANGROVE RIVER

SCOW

X CAMP

HALF-WAY TREE

TO OLD GOLDMINE

TRACK TO MANGROVE RIVER

THE MANGROVE SUMMER

Jack Lasenby

Auckland
OXFORD UNIVERSITY PRESS
Melbourne   Oxford

Oxford University Press

Oxford University Press, Walton Street, Oxford OX2 6DP

OXFORD   NEW YORK   TORONTO
DELHI   BOMBAY   CALCUTTA   MADRAS   KARACHI
PETALING JAYA   SINGAPORE   HONG KONG   TOKYO
NAIROBI   DAR ES SALAAM   CAPE TOWN
MELBOURNE   AUCKLAND
and associated companies in
BERLIN and IBADAN

Oxford is a trade mark of Oxford University Press

First published 1988
©Jack Lasenby 1988

The assistance of the New Zealand Literary Fund
is gratefully acknowledged

ISBN 0 19 558194 6

Cover illustration by Hilary Ravenscroft
Photoset in Baskerville by Rennies Illustrations Ltd.,
and printed in Hong Kong
Published by Oxford University Press
1A Matai Road, Greenlane, Auckland 3, New Zealand

CONTENTS

Book One
SUMMER AT THE BACH

CHAPTER ONE
The Japs Are Coming

THE SAME DAY THE JAPS bombed Pearl Harbour, we heard Dad was a prisoner of war.

Jimmy and I came home for lunch, and Mum was listening to the wireless. The cowardly attack had sunk most of the American battleships, it said, but the Yanks would now wipe out the Japanese.

I moved the kettle over the fire. As it began to sing, Jill galloped in. She always reckoned she never missed a day's high school, but she was home that day because she'd been down to the post office for the mail, I remember.

'It's about Dad!' she said, standing over Mum and pushing a letter at her.

Mum didn't want to open it. She looked at Jimmy, opened it very slowly, and read it to herself.

'What does it say?' Jill asked.

'Your father,' Mum said, 'he's a prisoner of war. In Germany.' Her hands folded the letter, put it back in its brown envelope, folded that, and tried to fold it again. Jill snatched it.

'He's wounded!' she read. 'We can write to him. The Red Cross will see he gets our letters.'

Mum didn't hear her. Her hands kept folding the letter that wasn't there, and she was crying. Jimmy started too.

'George, push the kettle over the fire,' Jill ordered. 'We'll have lunch.' I'd already made the tea, refilled the kettle, and put it on the back of the stove. 'They'll all want to know at school tomorrow, and I can tell them at Guides tonight.'

'You should be happy!' She swung on Jimmy. He was seven and had black curls Mum wouldn't cut. 'Dad's alive!' Jill shouted at him, but he cried all the more.

'Leave him alone, Jill,' Mum said. 'He's too little to understand.'

3

'The Japs are coming,' Jimmy snivelled.

Jill thought it unpatriotic to cry. 'Our father's alive, and you cry,' she said. 'That's just what Adolf Hitler wants.'

'How do you know what he wants?' I asked.

'Because they told us at Guides.' She turned to Mum. 'You'd better let Uncle Dugald know, and Aunty Iris and everyone at the Bay, and you'd better ring Uncle Paul and everybody up in Auckland. I'll pop over and tell the Campbells.'

'Just sit down and let me drink my tea, Jill,' Mum said, but she had already rung Uncle Dugald's number — long, short, long — on our line. Mum was still talking to him when it was time for Jimmy and me to go back to school.

When war broke out in 1939, Dad was one of the first to volunteer. I remember him coming in and saying, 'I've joined up.'

'You're drunk!' Mum said.

'Joined up. The army's going to make a man of me!' He laughed his easygoing laugh. Everybody liked Dad.

He wasn't like other kids' fathers. Mum blamed it on what she called the Slump, what they call the Depression now. 'There just weren't the jobs in the Slump,' she said, 'and there were you two to feed, then Jimmy came along, so your father started going off to the bush and bringing home meat. At least you never went hungry, not with that and his garden.'

Most of the men at home worked in the dairy factory. 'Your father couldn't stand a job like that,' Mum said. 'It would have·driven him crazy. I knew he was like that when I married him.'

Mr Campbell next door told Dad he was mad to join up.

'You're a married man with three kids, Stan. Let the single men go first.' Dad just grinned.

'Why risk your neck?' Mr Campbell went on. 'That Pommy Prime Minister Winston Churchill, he did his best to kill me at Gallipoli in the Great War. You watch out he doesn't try the same thing on you.'

Jill loved having a father in the Army. When Dad went off on the Rotorua Express to Auckland, after his final leave, she got dressed in her Guide uniform. I told her she thought she was being brave herself, and she flattened me. Jill was strong.

She knew everything about Dunkirk and the Battle of Britain. She listened to the news, read out the *Herald* to us, and cut out little flags and moved them around on a map of the world. She made the war sound boring.

I had a nightmare about a cartoon in the paper of Hitler as an octopus stretching his arms over all of Europe except Britain. Then we heard the Germans had beaten our men in Greece and Crete, and Mum got a letter saying Dad was missing, and his photo was in the *Herald*. Half the men in New Zealand seemed to be disappearing into the war, and there were long columns of names and photos:

Dead   Wounded   Missing

Mr Campbell told me it was that Winston Churchill again. 'Gallipoli last time, Greece this time,' he said. 'But you don't need to worry about your father, George. He's a survivor, like me.'

Germany attacked Russia and was winning there too. Mr Campbell said, 'Those slant-eyed yellow dogs, those Japs, they'll come in with Germany, and you watch out then!'

'No news of your father? Never mind,' he said. 'Stan's a survivor.'

That's when we heard Dad was missing.

Once, Jimmy said he couldn't remember what Dad looked like, so Jill stuck the photo of him in uniform over the mantelpiece, but the lemon-squeezer army hat made him look different. Mum had a photo of them when they got married, but that didn't look much like him either.

Jill seemed to think she was fighting Hitler all on her own. She got rigged up in her uniform and went off to Guides where they were runners for the Home Guard. She was always rolling bandages and making camouflage nets with a big wooden needle. Mum didn't say much about him, but Jill talked about Dad all the time. She

5

growled at Jimmy till he cried and she said he was unpatriotic for not remembering what Dad looked like.

When I told her Mr Campbell said the Russians were our best hope, Jill said, 'Mr Campbell had better be careful, or he'll be put in prison for communism. He doesn't even bother to black out his windows properly.'

'Mr Campbell was in the Great War. He was wounded at Gallipoli. He showed me his medals,' I said. 'And he's in the Home Guard.'

'Just the same, he'd better be careful. "Careless talk costs lives!" ' Jill loved quoting that poster.

'Mr Campbell's all right,' I said.

'They told us at Guides to keep an eye on people who talk like that,' Jill said. 'They're called fifth-columnists. Besides, he never goes to Anzac Day parades.'

But Uncle Dugald thought the same as Mr Campbell. 'If we wait for the Yanks to save us, we'll wait for ever,' he said. 'They didn't come into the Great War till it was nearly over. Those Russkis have got the right idea, with their scorched earth policy. The Huns will starve before they get to Moscow.'

Then Mrs Campbell said to Mum over a cup of tea one day, 'Those Commies in the coal mines, they'd get short shrift if they were in Russia. To think your Stan's missing, fighting for them, and they're on strike again. Some people don't know there's a war on.'

But Mum said later, 'Your father wouldn't have worked in the mines if they paid him in gold. He said the factory's bad enough, but fancy going down and working in the dark . . .' and Mr Campbell said, 'Too many accidents in the mines. Can't say I blame them for wanting better conditions.'

The only person who seemed to know exactly what she wanted and what she believed about everything was Jill.

And then, just a few weeks before Christmas 1941, we heard about Pearl Harbour, and Mum got the letter about Dad.

Two months later, the Japs had captured Singapore, and something terrible had happened to one of us. Now I'm a bit older, I can see how it all began that day with Jill bringing home the letter about Dad, and the man on the wireless telling us about the Japs coming into the war on Germany's side. Maybe it wouldn't have seemed so sad, if Dad had been all right. I know Jill thought she had to take his place, till he came home. She was always pretty bossy, Jill, and she never trusted Mum to look after us.

I wonder now if Jill missed Dad more than the rest of us did. Mum always said that when she was just a little thing Jill couldn't wait for him to come home, and he'd no sooner have taken off his boots at the back door than she'd have shoved her feet in them and would be clumping around, trying to look like him, and shouting orders at Brown, his dog. She was forever wearing his clothes, Mum said, his old cardigan, his hat, his coat. He couldn't take any of them off, but Jill would have them on.

Mum cried when the train took him away to the war, and so did Jimmy. But Jill didn't. In her Girl Guide uniform, she stood at the Matahina railway station — the train wouldn't stop at Waharua — and she saluted as Dad disappeared. Jill never cried at anything then. Poor Jill.

Anyway, I realize now that's when she must have decided she couldn't trust Mum any longer, that it was a good chance for her to take over the family and look after us till Dad came home. The Japs gave her the perfect excuse.

CHAPTER TWO
Going to the Bay

THAT NIGHT, MUM SAID, 'WE'RE going to the Bay.'
'Where will you get the benzene?' asked Jill.
'Never mind, I'll get it,' Mum said.
'They'll stop us along the road and send us home,' said Jill.
Mum snorted. 'I'd like to see anybody try to stop me. Your father's a prisoner of war, and nobody's going to stop his family going to the Bay for Christmas!'
I hoped she was right, because I loved the Bay. We all did. Even Jill wanted to go, but they'd said at Guides that people should help the war effort by not using their cars, so she had to have a growl.
Jimmy remembered the Bay. 'Will Derek be there?' he asked.
'Of course,' Mum said. 'And Graham, and Ann, and Aunty Iris.'
Mum was born in the Bay, and we went there every year. This had looked like being the first year we'd miss. Our cousins Graham, Ann, and Derek lived in Auckland with Uncle Paul. Their mother, Aunty Ann, was dead. Each year, we met at Aunty Iris's and went around to the bach. Ann was the one I wanted to see. We were all like one big family each summer.
After Dad went overseas, Mum bought a round-backed, green and black Morris 8 and taught herself to drive. Because benzene was rationed, she'd saved some in tins out in the car shed. We all knew it was there.
'Will Aunty Iris go up to Auckland for the others?' I asked.
'Perhaps they'll come down on the service car,' said Mum.
'If it's still running. They may not be allowed to travel,' Jill said.

'You're a real killjoy,' Mum told her.

'Well, there is a war on, you know.'

'Yes, Jill, we all know that.'

'Will we go to the bach?' I asked

'We'll see.'

'I remember the bach,' said Jimmy. 'I hope we go there.'

'I hope Ann's there,' I said. 'It wouldn't be like Christmas without her and the others.'

'Dad won't be having much of a Christmas in a prisoner of war camp,' Jill said, staring at Mum. She was much bigger than me. She was even taller than Mum.

'When he was on final leave,' Mum said, 'he told me to take you to the Bay each Christmas. He said we'd be safer there.'

'What if the Japs attack?' asked Jill.

'It'll be Auckland they attack, or Wellington, not the Bay. Your father said we could always take to the bush. Even the bach is well hidden from the sea.'

Mum said we weren't to tell anybody but Uncle Dugald and the Campbells.

'What about school?' asked Jill.

'Leave it to me,' Mum said.

It was exciting. We were going to the Bay, and we might go to the bach. Best of all, I was going to see Ann. And we were going before school finished!

We tore around for a couple of days getting everything ready. Mr Campbell changed the oil and greased the car for us. I helped him check the tyres and put a spot of rain water in the battery. Mrs Campbell said she'd look after our cat and feed the chooks. We were taking Brown, Dad's dog, with us in his box on the luggage carrier.

We packed the car one morning. The Campbells waved and wished us a merry Christmas, although it was still a few weeks away, and Jimmy, Brown, and I ran behind the car to Uncle Dugald's store. Don Hollis saw us and said, 'You'll get into trouble not going to school.' He was in my class. 'The Japs are coming,' he said. 'My mother says they'll be here before Christmas.'

Uncle Dugald filled our tank. Jill helped him pump the

9

benzene into the glass containers on the top of the pump, swinging the long handle to and fro. When they were full, he drained them down the hose into the tank. I like watching the benzene fill and empty, but its smell reminded me that I was always sick on the hill. Being carsick was the price I had to pay, going and coming back, for summer at the Bay. Ann was the only one who knew how I felt about it.

'Everybody's filling their tanks', said Uncle Dugald, 'and any spare tins they've got. The Government'll stop us selling soon.' He tied Brown's box on top of the suitcases on the luggage carrier. 'Tie up Brown,' he said, 'or he'll sneak off. I don't blame him. Damned if I'd like to go over the hill in that cage.'

Aunty Catherine had a cup of tea ready out the back of the shop. If grown-ups remembered being young, they'd know how long it takes them to do something like having a cup of tea or a chat. We had to try a piece of Aunty Catherine's Christmas cake, while they talked and talked, and Jill and Jimmy had a bottle of soft drink. Jimmy chose Green River, and the smell made me feel closed up in the car already. He looked at me, knew what I was thinking, and stuck his fingers down his throat, but Uncle Dugald saw him and clipped his ear.

'You two behave yourselves in the car,' he said. 'Your mother's got enough on her mind driving it. If you play up in the back, I'll thrash the pair of you when you come home. And keep away from the wharf, or I'll take my razor strop to you.'

'I hope you're doing the right thing, that's all,' Aunty Catherine was saying, 'going all that way when there's a war on.'

'Stan wanted us to go,' said Mum.

'All the same —'

'Of course he did!' said Uncle Dugald. 'You've got Jill to scare off the Japs. Now, you'd better get going, May, or it'll be dark before you get over the hill.' He caught up Brown, shoved him in his box, and tied down the lid. Jimmy and I rubbed Brown's nose and got in the back. Aunty Catherine gave me some P.K. gum and said, 'Chew it. It'll stop you being carsick.' I wished she hadn't reminded me. She gave the others bags of lollies.

Uncle Dugald shoved what looked like benzene coupons into Mum's hand. 'I know you've got enough,' he said, 'but take them just in case. Fill up at the Thames, and keep it filled at the Bay. You may just need to get away in a hurry if the news get any worse.'

Mum tooted, Brown barked, we all waved, and we were away.

Mum talked all the time she was driving. Our little car seemed to draw the farms past till we turned left before the war memorial in Te Aroha and drove north under the hills, the Waihou River on our left. Mum waved at the sandbanks and logs left by the floods. 'Look how green the paddocks are,' she said. 'They'll all be browned off when we come back, and the peat will be burning.'

Jill sat humped up, muttering, 'Keep your eyes on the road.' Jill wouldn't talk and look around at everything if she were driving. She wouldn't wave the way Mum did.

At a crossroads we had to stop for some soldiers. One stepped in front of the car. 'You can't go along here,' he said, and sounded pleased about it. 'The Army's doing an exercise, in case of the Japs.'

'There's nobody on the road now,' Mum said.

'I've got my orders,' the soldier said unpleasantly.

Mum tooted, revved the engine, and shouted, 'Get out of my way!' in a gruff voice we hadn't heard before. Brown set up a din on the back. The man jumped aside as Mum lurched forward. As we drove past them, the soldiers beside the road grinned and waved.

A few miles on we were stopped again. 'Where are you heading?' asked another soldier.

'Paeroa,' said Mum.

'From where?'

'Te Aroha.'

'All right, only this road's closed till tomorrow. Look, why don't you cut down here, take the second turn on your right, and it'll bring you back on the main road near

Paeroa, and you can go on to Thames,' he said. He grinned at Jimmy and me, perched on the towels and blankets, where we'd taken out the back seat to make room. 'Have a good holiday,' he laughed.

'You lied, Mum!' Jill said, as we drove on.

'He asked where we were heading, and I said Paeroa. He asked where we'd come from, and I said Te Aroha. I didn't lie,' Mum said. 'The cheek of that other one,' she went on, 'trying to tell me I can't use my own roads.'

'He was only trying to do his duty,' said Jill. 'We're not supposed to be travelling all that distance.' Her dark hair switched in the wind.

'Mum,' said Jimmy. 'Make Jill close her window.'

As we drove into Thames we could see mangroves, those strange trees that grow in the sea. Fishing nets hung drying; a few boats lay on their sides in the mud. There was no sign of the sea. When we stopped and filled up with benzene, the man said, 'You're in luck. I think they'll stop us selling to private motorists.'

We drove on over the hump in the middle of the main street, where a creek ran under the road. Mum waved her hand and asked if we remembered the time a log came down in a flood and jammed the culvert, and water poured over Pohlen Street. 'Your father was driving us down to the Bay', she said, 'in Uncle Dugald's old Essex.'

We went under the overhead conveyor at the disused gold mine and drove out of the north end of Thames, and there it was, like a dirty sheet hung against the sky: the sea! It went on and on, up into the sky, filling the world, as if it stood straight up. There were more fishing boats on their sides, and, somewhere beyond them, the mud and the sea become one.

'Good,' Jill said. 'The tide'll be in over at the Bay when we get there.' They were her first words for miles.

The road up the Thames coast was dusty. At Puru there was a bit of tar-seal, and people were walking along the grassy edge wearing togs and carrying towels. 'They don't look as if they know there's a war going on,' said Jill. It was true. Nobody looked as if they cared about anything.

The houses were small, overgrown with long grass and trees. The air was different: sharp and salty.

'Smell the sea!' Mum said, and Jimmy and I sniffed.

A pōhutukawa was just beginning to flower. Mum pointed at it and said, 'That's good luck for summer. They'll be coming out at the Bay.'

Along the side of the road, above a cliff, there was a log. Further on, in a narrow cutting, there was another. 'Tank traps!' said Jill. 'To stop the Japs. They told us about them at Guides. The Home Guard's going to swing them across and block the road.' She sounded pleased.

Where we turned off the coast and ran into the hills the road was narrower, the metal looser. Mum slowed. The car bumped over the corrugations, and Jimmy and I bounced in the back. Poor Brown gave a yowl.

'Hold on,' said Mum, 'here's another bad bit. The road's getting worse. There just aren't the men to maintain it.'

Where the creek spilled from pool to pool under the road, she pulled off and said, 'Let's have lunch. You can swim in the creek, and we'll let the service car get ahead of us.'

As usual, Jill took ages to shift herself, and I felt choked up by the time I could push her seat forward and get out. Jimmy let Brown out, and he looked dizzy for a moment, then barked and raced around the car.

He splashed in the creek with us, sneezed, coughed, and drank some water, and we copied him.

Mum lit a fire and boiled the billy. 'Don't you eat too much,' she said to me.

'Or you'll be sick,' said Jimmy.

'You'd better not have anything to drink,' Mum said.

'Or you'll be sick,' said Jimmy.

I watched them drink their tea and felt dry. Still, I'd swallowed a few mouthfuls of water in the creek.

'Before you get dressed, George,' Mum said, 'I'll tie some brown paper around your tummy.'

'What for?'

'It'll stop you getting carsick. Mrs Barker swears by it. She said it worked wonders with Freddy.' She wrapped a long length of wrapping paper round and round my middle. I crackled as I got into my clothes and it was hard to bend.

The others were calling Brown. Jimmy and I searched the creek, while Mum and Jill looked in the scrub across the road. They even drove back a couple of miles, in case he'd headed home. We looked for ages, but there was no Brown.

'He must be hiding,' said Mum. 'We'll just have to leave him. The service car'll be along soon, and I don't want to get too far behind it because it keeps the traffic off the road.

'Oh, where is that dratted dog? Give him another whistle, Jill.'

And Jill stuck her fingers in her mouth and whistled, as Dad had taught her, but there was no Brown.

Half a mile up the road there was a swing bridge across to a farm. Mum wrote a note asking the farmer to look after Brown if he turned up and gave Aunty Iris's address in the Bay. She stuck it in the kerosene tin they used for a letterbox. We were calling Brown for the last time, when the white service car with the red streak along its side went past with a toot, and we followed after the dust settled.

Jimmy cried as we got in the car and he grizzled away until Mum said the farmer was sure to find Brown and look after him. 'He'll enjoy helping look after the cows,' she said.

'Are there wild pigs here?' asked Jimmy.

'Lots! See, they've been rooting up there on the fern.'

'Mum!' shouted Jill. 'Keep your eyes on the road!'

'Brown'll be all right then,' said Jimmy, 'because Dad always said he was good on pigs,' but his face was still wet, and he looked back and cried again as we climbed.

'Promise we'll stop and look for Brown when we're coming home,' he said.

'I promise,' Mum said.

CHAPTER THREE
Carsick

THE ROAD CLIMBED AND WOUND in and out of corners and climbed and wound in and out again. It wasn't much more than two metalled wheel-tracks. The creek was on our left, a thousand feet below. On our right, the hills lifted into the sky. Once, we all looked back and saw the sea and some islands floating.

The banks were covered in ferns. Trees hung above. There were little waterfalls and creeks that crossed the road. 'The service car's not far ahead,' said Mum. 'See where it splashed water where it crossed this ford?' I didn't look. I was trying not to see, or hear, or feel anything.

'I wonder what Brown's doing?' asked Jimmy.

'Still hiding,' said Mum.

'Why?'

'Because he hates his box.'

I knew how he felt. The car was a steel box, and I was closed inside. I wanted to get out and hide too.

'He'll find the farm,' Mum said. 'There'll be some children who'll look after him. And Aunty Iris'll ask the service car driver to keep an eye out for him.

'Brown's a survivor,' she said.

I wished I was. The engine moaned around another bend, and my stomach moaned around with it. There was just corner after corner. Mum tooted at the sharper ones. The sound of the engine and the horn filled the world. I wanted to lie down in one of the fords and die. I didn't want to speak to anybody or look at anybody. I didn't want anybody to look at me. I just thought of the Bay.

'There we are,' Mum said, 'the top of the hill!' We climbed the last bit and pulled off beneath a sign that said 'Summit', and I pushed out past Jill, shoving her forward against the dashboard.

'Look out!' she yelled. 'Mum!' But I couldn't wait for

her to take her time getting out. She hit me, and I kicked her hard, then I was out and walking down the road away from the car and all of them. I pressed my face into the cold air. The bush disappeared in a light drizzle. I went on into the mist in the saddle. Suddenly I was sick in the middle of the road, bent over, vomiting and crying.

Around a corner, where a stream came down, I washed the sick out of my mouth and sat on a wet rock. The air was colder now. I liked it. I got up and walked on.

The Bay side was all downhill and easier for Mum, so she let me walk a long way. They coasted past me and stopped down a couple of bends where I caught up.

'Poo, you stink!' said Jimmy, as I got in. I couldn't even say I'd washed myself. 'I saw where you were sick in the middle of the road,' he said. 'We ran right over —'

'Be quiet, Jimmy!' Mum ordered. I looked at his black curls and bright eyes and wished he could be sick instead of me.

'It's dangerous, coasting downhill,' said Jill. 'They told us at Guides.'

'It saves benzene,' said Mum. I thought of its smell, and of Brown in his box, and had to get out and be sick again. Jill leapt out of the way this time, and I walked ahead again.

We went down the hill like that. They'd let me get ahead, pass me, pick me up, drop me again, and so on, all the way down to the roadman's house with the peach trees.

Mum said, 'Not long now, George,' but I didn't know what her words meant. 'The bush is drier down here,' she said. 'Just look at the dust!'

'I saw the service car,' Jill said. 'Miles below us, on a bend.' I didn't look down. I thought of Ann and wondered if she'd be there, and if Derek had got his nose sunburnt yet. He did, every year.

'Not too long to Gumtown now,' Mum said. I knew she was looking at me in the mirror, and I didn't look back. There were a couple of patchy paddocks with tumbledown fences disappearing into the bush. There was a swing bridge disappearing across a creek. It was somebody else seeing it, I thought, then realized Mum was saying, 'We're at the bottom of the hill now, George. That's the worst of it over!'

Ages later, Jill said, 'There's the river!' and I sat up and saw it, wide and still. The tide was creeping towards the mangroves.

'Not long now,' Mum said. I heard her saying the names, as she did every year: Slippery Crossing, Twin Bridges, Mill Creek, but I didn't care. I was too busy holding myself together.

And then, years later, we were there, and Aunty Iris was hugging us and saying, 'Where's Brown?' and I knew I'd paid for another summer at the Bay.

Aunty Iris lived in the house where she, and Mum, and Uncle Dugald, and Aunty Ann, and all their brothers and sisters had been born. It had a verandah around it, a hall down the middle with lots of bedrooms that were hardly used now, and a big kitchen out the back. Each summer, we filled it again, and the great trees our grandmother had planted leaned over it and listened to us talk.

Jill and Jimmy had disappeared. 'Come on,' said Aunty Iris. 'Get away from the car, George. You look a bit white still.'

Mum's old Morris 8 stood ticking in the gloom of the huge magnolia that spread over the front lawn. Its doors hung open, but it still looked hot. I didn't want to see it again, nor to think of all four of us packed inside. I looked at the magnolia instead, at the cool, creamy flowers riding high amongst its leaves, and smelled its richness, its deep scent that filled the lawn and house.

'Where's Ann?' I asked.

'They can't get on the service car,' said Aunty Iris. 'It's booked out all this week, so Uncle Paul's going to see if they can come down on the *Lady Jane*.'

'What if they can't?'

'We'll get them here somehow.'

'Dugald heard a rumour they're going to cancel the

trains,' said Mum. 'Something about the shortage of coal, and the strikes in the mines. They can't stop everything, surely.'

I followed Aunty Iris along the dark hall, through the door with coloured glass, and into the kitchen, and lay down in the little bedroom off that. I must have slept because I woke and heard them talking about the Japanese.

'Dugald's sure they're coming,' Mum was saying.

'Yes,' said Aunty Iris. 'Did you see those great logs the Army's put along the coast?'

'Jill knew they're tank traps,' said Mum. 'But surely the Japs will attack Auckland first.'

I was waking up. I felt better. I was at the Bay! As I went into the kitchen, Jimmy ran in saying the dinghy was afloat.

'We've been watching Luke Kelly pick up his mooring,' he said. 'He's just come in, and there're seagulls all around his boat. Jill says can we go for a row?'

'Of course,' Aunty Iris said. 'Here, take these sandwiches.'

'So you're on your feet again,' Mum said to me. 'Do you feel like eating something?'

I took the sandwiches, I was starving, and ran after Jimmy. 'I'm coming too! Wait for me!'

'You'd better not do any running, George!' Mum called, but I was running through the orchard, smelling the trees. Then the shells were crunching sharp under my feet, and I was standing in salt water, smelling the river, and listening to the gulls cry. The tide was coming in across the pipi banks, carrying the smell of the sea. We pushed off the dinghy, jumped in, and Jill rowed out through the channel across the bank and on to the river.

'We could hide up the river if the Japs come,' I said.

'We'd need a lot of food,' said Jill. 'Tents, a net, billies, an axe, fishing lines. We'd need all sorts of things. Spears, a camp oven, spare clothes . . .' She was staring down into the bottom of the boat, pulling hard on the oars. Her dark hair swung forward and hid her face, but I knew she'd been planning. Jill always planned things ahead.

It was late when we anchored on the side of the channel and crunched across the pipi shells. We had tea, and I went to bed. The others stayed up talking in the kitchen.

I didn't hear the nine o'clock news, but woke just enough to hear Big Ben chiming away across the world in London, and thought how Jill would be telling the others to pray during the silence that followed, just as she'd have everybody on their feet whenever the wireless played 'God Save the King'. I sank down into sleep again, pleased I wasn't there. That's why I didn't hear the announcement that half the trains from Auckland were cancelled, travel was limited, and selling benzene was forbidden.

Next morning, we'd hear the mayor of Auckland was encouraging mothers with families to travel before Christmas, to take the load off public transport. Later there'd be an announcement that schools would close early to spread the rush.

I'd hear it all next morning, but, as Big Ben boomed for the nine o'clock news, I woke, thought, 'We're at the Bay. Ann and the others are coming too,' and felt we'd escaped something, then must have slept again.

CHAPTER FOUR
The Hill-Billies

I CREPT OVER THE LAWN under the darkness of the magnolia next morning and heard again the sound that had wakened me, a voice calling an order. The light was misty on the road. People were tramping. Then they loomed out of the mist: men and horses.

The men were in uniform and each led several horses. Their boots struck against the road, the horses' hooves clopped together in a long drum roll, and there was a high tinkling sound, a sort of ringing.

I stood at the gate with the brass latch that had come off a wrecked sailing ship a century ago. One of the men saw me, grinned and winked, and called, 'Good-day, young George!'

'Hallo Tim!' It was my youngest uncle.

'So you got here! Tell May I'll try to nick in later.' He nodded, winked, and was gone, and I saw he was wearing spurs. That's where the ringing came from.

I felt the cool brass latch in my hand, dropped it, and ran back under the tree and down to the beach. The tide was low. The dinghy lay on her side. The sun was burning the last mist off the water. The gulls had flown out to sea. I crunched across the pipi shells towards the old wharf, high on its spindly, criss-crossed legs.

As I dug after a crab, my name floated on the air. Jimmy called, 'Mum says you've got to come and have your breakfast.'

I'd seen the *Lady Jane* wasn't at the new wharf. Sometimes she sneaked in early. If the others were coming, they wouldn't be in for a couple of hours now, so I raced Jimmy up to the house.

'I saw Tim dressed as a soldier,' I said. 'They were wearing spurs and leading horses down the road.'

'The Mounted Rifles are in camp,' said Aunty Iris, putting

things on the table. 'Jill, cut some bread, and you finish setting the table, George. Did you throw some wheat to the chooks, Jimmy? Just one scoop.

'Yes,' she went on, 'they've commandeered the hall for their barracks. Tim joined them.'

'Tim!' Mum said.

'I saw him!' I said. 'He's going to call in later.'

'Mounted Rifles? What are they?' Mum asked.

'Mainly locals,' said Aunty Iris. 'Come on, George, you and Jimmy slip in around the other side. Help yourself to fritters. I got the mussels across at the point.

'A sort of cavalry,' she said to Mum. 'Jill, here's your plate. That's it. Now, there's an egg each for you.

'They ride up and down the coast, patrolling it, and they've a look-out on Maungawhero. Tim says they can see right out past the islands. I think they're supposed to work in with the Home Guard and the Army.'

'I can't see Tim doing much,' Mum said. 'He'll be too busy skylarking, if I know him.'

'Well, he did say they spend a lot of time pig hunting, but he was always one to talk, wasn't he!

'Eat up, George,' Aunty Iris said. 'You need to fill up after yesterday.'

'Are the others coming?' I asked.

'Uncle Paul rang last night, just before the exchange closed. They're on the *Lady Jane*, but she left late and had to call in at the Barrier, so they won't be in till midday. There, I knew that'd take the long look off your face!

'Now, let's get things cleaned up, and we can go and meet them.'

We did the dishes, raked the magnolia leaves and carted them down to the orchard, went to the shops for Aunty Iris, and filled ourselves with plums. When it was time to go, Jill and I took the dinghy.

I rowed, and we went along the edge of the pipi banks, under the end of the old wharf, and across the sandy bank towards the new wharf.

'Don't wave them in the air,' Jill said, looking at the

oars. 'It's easier, if you feather them,' and she grabbed my hands and turned the blades as I swung back.

'Leave me alone!'

'Come on! Row! She's coming in. The others are waving. Here, you'd better give me the oars!'

I'd have told her to shut up, but didn't have the breath. We anchored the dinghy carefully because the tide was coming in, and raced up the wharf. The *Lady Jane* was surging in with the tide around the point. We could hear her rumbling. Now she was swinging around and coming into the wharf, slowing against the current. A rope went around a pile. I could see Captain Creed spinning the wheel. There was a sudden rumble and a flurry of water. Lines went up, and Jill dropped one over a bollard. Aunty Iris did the same with the stern line. The engine quietened and ticked smoothly. The *Lady Jane* was alongside, her derrick already swung out ready to start unloading.

At her white-painted masthead, where the wind-vane used to be, a model Spitfire pointed into the wind, its propeller just turning over. The lifeboat on the davits at the stern was still a bright blue, but the *Lady Jane's* hull was grey .

And there, hanging on to the varnished rail beside the wheelhouse, was Graham, and Derek, and there was Ann. I grinned at them and looked away when Ann smiled and called my name. Then they were over the rail and jumping on the stringer along the wharf, and Mum was saying, 'Wait for the gangway,' and they were letting Aunty Iris and Mum kiss them, then turning and looking at us, and we were standing looking at them as if we'd never seen each other before.

'Just made it, they did,' Captain Creed was saying, and I was still looking at Ann, grinning and saying hallo all at once. 'Paul brought them down, just as we were about to sail. He gave me this letter for you.'

We had a look in the cabin, at the bunks and brass portholes. 'Lucky pigs!' I said to Ann.

'You wouldn't have liked it,' she said. 'There was a big swell off Colville. We had to run into Tryphena to drop somebody, then we picked up the swell again, coming down the coast. Were you very sick?'

I nodded.

'All over the hill!' said Jimmy. 'He was sick all over the road. Lucky it's rained ever since we came through.'

'I thought of you,' Ann said. 'I kept sending thoughts, trying to help you.'

'Where's Brown?' Derek asked. We were carrying their bags down the wharf. I looked and saw his nose was sunburnt.

'Brown's lost,' I said, and Jimmy looked as if he'd cry.

'I know the place,' Ann said, when I told them about it. 'Remember, we all had a swim and lunch there, the time Aunty Iris drove us down and we met at Thames. There were some kids from the farm playing on the swing bridge. They'll find Brown and look after him.'

Things always seemed better when Ann was there. Jimmy forgot about crying and told her how he'd taught Brown to beg, and she listened to him carefully and said he was clever.

We rowed back with all their stuff, Ann and I perched in the stern among the bags and cases. The tide was further in, but we still had to cross a bit of pipi bank, and our cousins hopped and danced across the shells.

'Townie feet!' said Jill, as we carried their stuff ashore, and they sat and put on sandals.

'Have you had a letter from Uncle Stan?' Graham asked.

'Not yet, but Uncle Dugald's going to send on any mail. Mum said Dad couldn't write himself because he's wounded.'

'There was a convoy getting ready to leave, when we came out,' said Graham. 'There were warships over at Devonport, and more waiting outside. It looked like a couple of troop ships were in at the wharves. There must be more men going overseas.'

'They're building a submarine net right across the harbour,' said Derek, 'and . . . and . . .' He got excited and tripped over his words. 'And Captain Creed said there's going to be guns and searchlights at each end. He thinks the Japs might attack us.'

'Are we going to the bach?' Ann asked.

'Nobody's made up their mind yet,' Jill said. 'Tim's in the Mounted Rifles.'

They all wanted to know what they were.

'Just Tim and all the farmers on their horses. They're supposed to be cavalry,' Jill snorted. 'I can't see them stopping the Japs.'

'We had a mock air raid in Auckland,' said Derek, 'with . . . with planes!'

'They dropped smoke bombs in the railway yards,' said Graham. The Army and the Home Guard and the E.P.S. all rushed round, getting in each other's way. We carried messages, the Scouts and Guides. It was a mess!'

'We had black-out tests too. Somebody reckoned they had a plane up reporting lights. It's stupid, because all the lights are on all night down on the waterfront.'

'Do you have the black-out?' Ann asked me. 'I don't like it.'

'Ann got chased by a drunk,' said Derek. 'Off the tram.'

'Oh, shut up,' said Ann, but Derek went on chanting it.

'Ann got chased by a drunk. Ann's boyfriend's a drunk!'

'What happened?' Jill asked.

'I was coming home after Guides. I got off the back platform, at our stop, and a soldier got off and chased me, once the tram had gone. There weren't any street lights, because of the black-out.'

'What happened?'

'Nothing. I just ran and got away, but it happened again, so Dad said that was it, no more Guides. I was getting sick of it anyway.'

'Was it the same soldier?' Jill asked.

'I don't know. The trams have very dim lights now, because of the black-out . . .'

'Dad got on to the police, but they told him there's nothing much they can do about it,' said Graham. 'It's easy to get away with things in the black-out.'

'We carry messages for the Home Guard,' said Jill. 'They do exercises all the time, up home. We've got the best Home Guard in New Zealand.'

'Uncle Dugald's an officer,' said Jimmy, 'but I heard him telling Mum he's more scared of the Home Guard than he is of the Japs.'

'What do you do if you're late going home now?' I asked Ann.

'I ring Dad, and he meets me. And you always get off the front platform, never the back.'

'Come on. Lunch is waiting for you!' It was Aunty Iris calling from the orchard.

Next day, we watched the *Lady Jane* loading slings of butter. She'd been up the river, unloaded some cargo there, and come down with the tide. Now she was nearly ready to start back for Auckland. We watched the crew fasten the big hatch, with its canvas cover battened down. Captain Creed checked the wedges driven in around it himself.

We dropped the mooring lines for them. As water boiled from the stern, and the bow swung out from the wharf, Captain Creed came level with us, just a few feet away. 'Have a good time at the bach!' he called, and the *Lady Jane* was on her way, the Spitfire turning into the wind, its propeller spinning in a blur.

We ran the whole way home and charged in, lifting the brass latch on the gate, rushing under the magnolia, tearing up the hall, and bursting into the kitchen.

'Captain Creed said we're going to the bach!' we all shouted and stood panting.

'Yes,' Aunty Iris admitted. 'We're going to the bach.'

'When? When?'

'Tomorrow.'

'If you let us get all this cooking done,' said Mum.

We jumped around the kitchen.

'We looked across at Whalers Beach and hoped!' yelled Graham.

'Dad said we weren't to bother you, but we've been hoping you'd take us there,' said Ann. 'Dad said we'd be safer there than in the Bay if the Japs came.'

'We thought it'd be better.' Aunty Iris looked at Mum. 'There's no pictures this year, with the Mounted Rifles using the hall, and there's no benzene for the cars, so we might as well go to the bach. But we're not going because of the Japanese.'

'Luke Kelly's going to drop us off tomorrow.'

'We'll help get things ready!'

Aunty Iris smiled. 'There's nothing much,' she said. 'I had most things ready and was just waiting for you all to arrive.

'Graham, you make sure the dinghy's where she'll be afloat in the morning. You can pick all the ripe plums. We'll take all the cabbages and lettuces that are ready, but that can wait for the morning.'

Tim called in that afternoon. He kissed Mum and laughed at all of us. His face was brown under a broad, flat-topped hat.

'So, how are the Mounted Rifles?' Mum asked.

'The Hill-Billies?' he said. 'Oh, we're good for a laugh. The horses are pretty fit, and we've scared a few pigs. I don't know if we'll scare the Japs. They could laugh themselves to death when they see us . . .' Tim always had to make a joke of everything.

He said he might see us at the bach because they rode patrols out to the Mangrove River occasionally. Then he heard something, his mates returning, and ran down the path, vaulted the gate without opening the latch, and joined the soldiers tramping back to the barracks. We ran and saw the sergeant pretending not to see him rejoining them.

'I'd hate to see them trying to stop the Japs,' said Graham.

'Why?' said Jill. 'Our men are better than the Japs.'

'Have you been listening to the news?' Graham said, as the sound of boots and spurs faded. 'Dad says they'll be in Singapore soon after Christmas at the rate they're going. They could attack Australia and New Zealand in the New Year. That's why he thinks we're safer here than in Auckland.'

CHAPTER FIVE
The Bach

W E STARTED EARLY. BY THE time Luke Kelly rowed out, we had everything aboard his boat, the *Idalia*. He had skin like the bark of a tree from working at sea all his life. When he laughed his eyes disappeared in wrinkles.

'Get up on the bow,' he told Graham and Jill, 'and be ready to drop the buoy,' and he went to start the motor.

As we went past the wharf, towing the dinghy, its mast and sails lashed inside, Ann sniffed and grinned. Luke Kelly's boat always smelled of fish. She looked at some people on the wharf watching us. 'They'll be wondering where we're off to, and wishing they were us,' she said.

It only took a couple of hours. Graham and Jill steered. They were always allowed to do things like that because they were the eldest. We crept along beneath Maungawhero, past Whauwhau Beach, saw Lost Bay and its beautiful sand among the cliffs, and rode the swell off Whalers Beach. We knelt in the cockpit and pointed at the mouth of the creek and the top of the fort. Ann squeezed my hand and danced around the cockpit, and we all shouted, 'We're back! We're back!' Even Luke Kelly had a grin, and his eyes disappeared.

Aunty Iris and Graham got into the dinghy, then Ann and me. Luke Kelly and Mum handed down bags and boxes of gear, then we fell away from the *Idalia* and rode down the back of one of the breakers that marched in to pound on Whalers Beach. It slipped away beneath us. The dinghy hung a moment. Aunty Iris and Graham dug in their oars, and we shot in on another breaker. Ann and I hung on to each other and laughed. We'd landed through surf before, but it was always exciting.

Off the mouth of the creek, beside the cliffs, the water was smoother. We shot in on a wave that didn't break and were suddenly floating up the creek. Aunty Iris and

Graham pulled up to the bend. Ann shoved me, and I knew what she was looking at, but I had my eyes closed.

'Go on,' she said, 'you can open them now.'

I did so. We were coming around the bend, the rock above us, a pōhutukawa hanging out from it, and red stamens floating down as we slid silently through its shadow. Graham and Aunty Iris were resting their oars. I could hear the drip of water from the blades, as they looked over their shoulders.

'It's still there!' Ann said.

There, standing on long, rickety legs right out into the creek, was the bach.

It was one huge room with a verandah the same size out over the water. We came alongside the steps, and Ann and I were up them in a flash, running our hands along the verandah rail, sitting on the forms around the big table.

'Open up!' Aunty Iris called and threw me the key. We unlocked the door and ran in together. There were bunks around three walls. Ann and I jumped on two top ones. 'Bags this one!' we shouted together.

There was the fireplace, there were the stools, there were the two chairs made out of barrels. We plonked ourselves down in them and grinned at each other. 'Smell the rum!' I said, and Ann went all drunk and rolled on the floor.

'There are our fishing lines!' she said. Lines, bottles, knives, boxes, tins, files, books, hooks, hammers, sinkers, jars of nails and screws, packets of matches, candles, and all the other things you need in a bach stood on the noggins between the studs. There were spare rowlocks, feathers, pāua shells, crab shells, coloured stones, a gannet's skull, bits of kauri gum, all the odds and ends of other summers.

A sack curtain cut off the bunk end of the bach. At the other end was the open fireplace, a bench with a sink, two crates of blankets and old clothes, some shelves of billies, mugs, plates, knives, forks, and spoons, and that was it.

Ann was jiggling from one foot to the other. 'We're back!' she said, and she kissed me, and the bunks, and the door, and the table on the verandah, and Aunty Iris who was trying to shove the mast and the rudder and centreboard up the steps over everything else she'd dumped there.

'Now, love,' she said, heaving them on to the verandah and hugging Ann in return, 'you and George get all this gear up the steps. But first, I want you to go up and clean out the waterfall, all the leaves and rubbish. Get it running clear, and put the spout in. We'll need a cup of tea by the time we get everything ashore!'

'Come on!' I said, and we were out of the back door, up the track, across the plank over the stream, and up to the big rock where we dug out the leaves and fallen branches and watched the little waterfall run clear. I jammed the spout back in place, while Ann got a billy. We stuck our mouths under the spout and tasted the water, cold and clear.

'It tastes good!' we spluttered at each other. We filled the billy, tipped it out, filled it again, and bolted back, not spilling it.

'You light it!' I said, and Ann knelt in front of the dry tea-tree twigs in the fireplace.

'Bach fire, we light you again!' she said, as we'd said every summer that we could remember, and put a match to the twigs. As we fed it heavier sticks, there was a yell. I hung the billy over the flames, and we ran to heave the gear off the steps and on to the verandah, just before Graham was back, rowing with Jill, and with Mum in the stern.

'You've got the fire going. That's nice!' Mum said.

'Ann and I've bagsed the top bunks on this side,' I said, tying the painter to the steps with a bowline.

'We'll see about that,' Jill said. She pushed past and careered inside. We helped Graham unload, and pushed him off. He said he could get back alone.

By the last trip, we'd had a swim in the creek, the billy had boiled, and Mum had lunch ready on the verandah.

We chewed thick meat sandwiches, gulped tea from mugs, and watched the tide turn. 'There!' said Ann. The red patch on the water beneath the pōhutukawa slipped towards the mouth of the creek.

'Why didn't Luke Kelly come in for lunch?' asked Derek. He looked more sunburnt than ever. I noticed he and Jimmy were exactly the same height.

'There's too much of a swell out there, and he might drag,' said Jill.

'He's off to pick up his pots,' Aunty Iris said. 'He might drop in some crayfish tomorrow, so keep an eye out for him.' She was rolling herself a cigarette. We all watched because most women smoked only tailor-mades. She licked it down, lit it, and waxed the end with a match, all in one movement. Derek took the wax match and threw it smoking into the creek.

'You used to tell us you could blow smoke out of your ears,' Jimmy said.

'So I can,' Aunty Iris said. 'Oh,' she sighed, 'it's good to be here!'

Jill had untied my bowline and tied another, so I undid hers and tied my own again. She and Graham had set up the mast, so it rode beside the verandah. Our towels hung along the rail like flags. We were back, all of us together!

Mum said we couldn't swim till we'd digested our lunch, so we rowed across the creek and climbed into the sand-hills. 'Wait for us!' Jimmy and Derek cried like seagulls, but Jill and Graham plunged on and disappeared. Ann and I followed, leaping into space and splashing down in the sand beside them just before Jimmy and Derek came flying and tumbling after us.

The jumping pit always stayed deep and steep-sided. Graham reckoned the wind whirled in it like a big drill, lifting out the sand. It was hard climbing out. We pulled each other back, rolled down, and had to start again. Jill didn't like it when I pulled her down, but she'd pulled Graham twice, so I threw sand in her face when she kicked me. That made her mad, but I was above her and kept there. We climbed, slid, climbed again, and, at last, we all stood on top of the fort.

Beyond, there were miles of sand-hills rippling like another sea all the way to the Mangrove River at the other end of Whalers Beach, covered in marram grass and lupin; miles of sand-hills, curved and sculptured by the wind, pointed and smoothed, jumping, slumping, tottering, blowing, stinging, leaping, falling, yelling and shoving sand-hills. And it was all our own for another summer, our kingdom by the sea.

Years ago, two older cousins, Rod and Tony, had started building a fort on the tallest sand-hill. They were both overseas now, in the Air Force and the Army. Rod had been wounded and was coming home for Christmas. We'd gone on building the fort they'd begun. It had sandbag walls around the top, with gaps to take our driftwood cannon. It took us days to drag one big log to the top.

We had a guardhouse with sandbag walls, and a rusty roof of corrugated iron, and a chimney. Like the rest of the fort, it was full of sand. When we started throwing it out with our hands, Graham said we needed a shovel. 'We'll get some planks,' he said. 'They'll do.'

But we went on, throwing it out with our hands. That's how I found the oilskin bag buried in the floor of the guardhouse.

'Give me that!' Jill snatched it.

'Give it back!' But she'd opened it. Several shiny things dropped, and Jimmy and Derek felt in the loose sand and found them: bullets!

'Look at this!' Jill held a map of the coast from Mangrove River into the Bay itself. It showed the sand-hills, our fort, the bach, even our track over the hills and the main track down the Whauwhau Beach and into the Bay. It showed the creek, Lost Bay, the cliffs, and, right on top of Maungawhero's bluffs, a spot marked 'Mounted Rifles Look-out'.

The boys wouldn't open their hands, but Jill just squeezed Derek's fingers down till he yelped and opened them. 'They're twenty-twos,' she said.

31

'What did you expect?'

'Well, whoever made the map must be a spy,' she said 'so I thought they'd have a Jap gun.'

'What's this?' Graham was looking at some scribbles down the side of the map.

'Japanese writing,' said Jill. 'They showed us some at Guides, so we'd know it.'

'It could just be scribbling,' said Ann.

Of course it couldn't be the Japs. We were in our fort, above the jumping pit, across from the bach, where Mum and Aunty Iris were probably having forty winks, or sitting on the steps with their feet in the water, drinking tea, and talking about the old days, the way they always did. The sun had gone out, and a cold breeze blew across the sand-hills. I looked at Ann.

'If the Japs come', said Jill, 'we're finished. I've been listening to the news, and it's all bad.' She sounded pleased. 'Mum and Aunty Iris don't think we can defend ourselves, because most of our soldiers are fighting in the Desert. I think New Zealand will just surrender if the Japs come.'

'I thought you said our men were better than the Japs?' said Graham. He didn't often challenge Jill, although he was the same age.

'They are too, but most are overseas. All the best of them.'

'What about the Mounted Rifles?' said Graham. 'And the Home Guard? You said you saw tank traps along the Thames coast. They're better than nothing. Look out there: those are our ships!'

Hull down, several ships steamed east, just their masts and funnels showing.

'That's the convoy you saw in Auckland,' said Jill. 'More of our men going overseas. We've got hardly any ships of our own, and no planes. The Japs could just land and take us over tomorrow.'

'The Yanks would stop them,' said Graham.

'The Yanks aren't here. They're too busy trying to refloat their battleships after Pearl Harbour.'

She climbed the parapet and slid towards the beach.

We followed her in a long line. A continuous roar like a train came from the far end of Whalers Beach, rumbled past us, and snored away to the mouth of the creek, as a wave curled, collapsed, swished up the sand, and withdrew. And somewhere out there over the horizon, the Japs were coming.

We raced up and down between waves, trying to keep in front of them without getting our feet wet. Jimmy slipped, and a wave swept up and covered him. Ann and I caught him and hung on, water up to our waists. It tried to suck us back into the sea. As it went down, Ann yelled, 'Run!' and Jimmy bolted up the beach.

'Fools!' Jill said. 'If you get swept out here, the undertow could get you.

'Don't any of you say anything to Mum and Aunty Iris about the map!'

'I think we should show them,' said Ann.

Jill swung on her so suddenly that Ann stepped back against me. She still held my hand from running up the beach, and I felt her fingers tighten as Jill hissed, 'Don't you dare!'

We were all quiet. It was a few days before Christmas. Up the creek, the dinghy lay dry. Mum and Aunty Iris were sitting in the shade on the verandah. They waved, but kept talking. The rocks beneath the pōhutukawa were red.

'Oh, Catherine didn't think we should be coming,' Mum said, as we climbed the steps.

'Why ever not?'

'Oh, you know her. She's a proper killjoy. She had the cheek to say to me, "There's a war on, you know," as if I didn't know.'

'Come on,' Aunty Iris said, 'we'll have a cup of tea and go for a walk along the beach.'

We dumped ourselves around the table. They didn't see the oilskin bag Jill took inside and hid in her bunk, while Graham disappeared under the bach, looking for a plank to make into a shovel.

CHAPTER SIX
The Spy

I WOKE THAT NIGHT TO hear the murmur of voices from the verandah. Our bunks were chaff sacks split open and nailed to heavy frames. It was hard to get out, but I did so without waking anybody, slipped through the curtain, and stood inside the door.

'We couldn't survive,' Mum was saying. 'We'd need tents, clothes, food . . .'

'We've got plenty of everything but food,' Aunty Iris said. 'All we need's a load of stores from the Bay. Besides, there must be something to eat in the bush.'

'A few berries and fern shoots. Pigs. Eels. It'd be hard going,' said Mum. 'And what if the kids fell ill?'

Aunty Iris said, 'It might be better than what could happen to them if we took them home.'

'It's the girls I'm worried about. Did you read in the *Herald* what the Japs did to those nurses?'

'Rape? But, surely —'

'Of course they would. They're like animals. You've read what the papers say about them, and you know what they look like.'

'Who's that?'

The floor must have creaked under me, so I stumbled out saying I wanted a drink of water.

Back in my bunk, I slid down into sleep. Far away there was the crash of surf.

Ann woke me, tickling my foot. It was still dark, but the door was a lighter shape. Somebody stirred as we slipped out and took the flounder spears from under the bach. There was enough water to cover the big flat upstream.

I missed the first one. It took off in a flurry of sand past Ann. She got it, as I speared another which hadn't moved. We slid them up the spears with our toes, and dropped them into the sugar-bag pīkau on my back.

Ann got most of them. We had seven when we turned back. Smoke rose among the trees. The sun shone. We splashed around the last corner, yelling and waving the pīkau.

Mum fried them, while we ran up and washed under the waterfall. Jill and Graham were chopping tea-tree.

'Take a decent load down with you,' said Jill.

'What's rape?' I asked her.

'You talk dirty and I'll tell Mum,' she said, and went ahead with an armload.

Mum switched me around the legs with a stick as I went inside. 'Don't you dare say rude things to your sister,' she said.

'I didn't!'

'I know what you were up to,' she said, and gave me a couple more.

Nobody looked at me as I went to my place at the table. Ann put a piece of bread on my plate, but I looked at my flatty and didn't feel like eating it. Jill picked the roe out of hers, lifted it slowly, put it in her mouth, and chewed it. She looked at me and smacked her lips.

'Try this one as well,' I said, and turned my plate upside-down on her head. I leapt down the steps, around the bach, and up the track to the cliffs. Jill would be after me, but I'd heard Ann stand and shove back the table, giving me a start. I climbed into the bush above the track and hid. Seconds later, Jill pounded past, going like a horse. I moved higher into the trees.

She came thundering back, a few minutes later, to search the other track. I slid down and followed the cliff track to where I could see the mouth of the creek and Whalers Beach as far as the mouth of the Mangrove River. As I looked there, a smudge of smoke blossomed and disappeared.

The track got higher. It wasn't fair what Jill did. Below me now there was the fish hospital, a huge hole where the roof of a cave had dropped in, leaving an arched bridge. We thought sick fish went in there to recover, and often rowed past it, but it was too dangerous to go near.

Mum always listened to Jill because she was the eldest. It wasn't fair. If Mum hit me Jill always used it as an excuse to join in. I hated them all.

I slid down to the beginning of the arch. A wave slopped into the chamber below, lifted towards me with a gulp, and surged out again. There were no fish, it was full of rocks and seaweed. I straddled the arch and pulled myself up. Another wave boiled below. It boomed, and an invisible hand of air pushed against me. I hung on and saw the seaweed open and close long arms.

The arch trembled each time a wave thundered in. I clung to the top and shuffled myself over. It was harder going down. I had to stand to get around two little bushes. Somebody yelled, and I almost let go.

I sat with a bump, grabbed the stone arch with my legs and arms, and saw Jimmy and Derek on the beach. They looked tiny, but I could see them waving. Ann ran towards them from the mouth of the creek. I stood, worked past the bushes, stumbled down the other side, and climbed towards the track.

My knees shook when I stopped, so I sat and hugged them. When I stood again, Ann waved. I waved back, climbed, and pulled myself through a gap in the tea-tree. Everywhere else, it was a solid wall, packed hard and cut off flat on top by the wind. I passed between grey slabs of stone, and went down the track under the pōhutukawa, sliding and running out on to the shiny beach of Lost Bay.

It wasn't sand. I ran it through my fingers: millions of tiny bits of shell, smooth and bright, polished by the sea. It glistened and sparkled where the waves drew back.

I shouted and jumped along the steep beach, beating the waves. At the far end, I crawled through the cave and climbed out on the rocks, where I tore off mussels, filling my shirt with them. I got too many and had to take off my shirt and carry it like a kit, back to an old shack, half-way along the beach. It stood among flax by a tiny creek.

A young man sat by the fireplace under the pōhutukawa. Smoke drifted from the ashes. I must have run past without seeing him.

'Catching your breakfast?'

'Yes.' I didn't say it was the second time that morning.

His name was Simon. He'd stayed in the old shack a couple of days. As I got the fire going again and cooked the mussels on a bit of corrugated iron, Simon made a billy of tea. We ate the bright orange flesh, as the mussels opened, and shared his mug.

He was on his way to join up. He was too young, so he'd have to put up his age. There mightn't be another chance, he said, so he was having this last tramp along the coast.

'We think there's a Jap spy here,' I told him.

'Why?'

'We found a map and some bullets in our fort.'

'I'm your spy,' Simon grinned. 'I left the map and bullets there so I could come back after the war and find them. I thought the fort was deserted.'

'Have you got a rifle?'

'A twenty-two. I've shot a couple of rabbits for a change from mussels.'

Simon said he must be going. He wanted to get into the Bay so he could catch the service car over to the Thames next morning. He climbed up the steps cut in the rock cliff behind the shack and disappeared around a bluff with his pack and rifle. I felt lonely. I'd forgotten about running away.

He'd left nothing behind. The shack was swept clean with a tea-tree branch. There was some driftwood inside the door for firewood. The shutter that did for a window was coming loose, and the door didn't shut properly. I was sitting, feeding sticks and dead leaves on the fire, when Jill and Graham arrived.

'What do you think you're doing?' Jill shouted, grabbing my arm. 'We've been hunting everywhere for you.'

37

She shoved me, bellowed, and called me names, and I just sat there and said nothing, knowing she'd quieten down, and she did, growling away again every few minutes, but slowly losing interest.

She was a bit like a dog, I thought.

'How'd you light the fire?' Graham asked.

'It was going.'

'Liar!' Jill said.

I didn't explain. I got a telling-off from Mum when we got back. Aunty Iris said nothing.

The others spent the afternoon digging out the fort, jumping, and swimming. I had to stay around the bach. Derek couldn't go across to the fort because he'd got sunburnt, and we played on the grassy patch at the foot of the track. Ann came up, and Jimmy too. Finally, Mum let us go for a swim, only Derek had to keep his shirt on.

'And keep your heads wet,' Mum said, 'or else wear your hats while you're in the water. Some people say it's the sun gives you infantile paralysis.'

None of us wanted to be cripples, so we kept ducking our heads under. The creek was warm and there were shoals of sprats.

The days slipped by like the tides, running into each other. Jill kept looking for the Japanese spy. When we had a picnic at Lost Bay, the sand was smooth, the shack empty. We caught snapper off the rocks, had a feed of mussels, and returned to the bach, tired, sunburnt, pleased to see the roof beneath us. Ann and I carried a kitful of mussels, and they were getting heavy. Smoke rose from the chimney.

Tim sat inside, making himself a cup of tea. 'Good-day, you lot,' he said.

'Tim!' we yelled.

'How are things at the Bay?' Aunty Iris asked.

'I checked the house,' he said. 'Everything's OK, and the chooks are laying. There's only one thing wrong.' We all looked at him.

'The pub's going to be out of beer for Christmas!

'I've brought your mail and the papers.' He nodded at the table. 'Nothing from Stan yet, May,' he said to Mum.

Still, there was a letter from Uncle Dugald saying our house was all right; Mr and Mrs Campbell sent their best wishes; everything was fine, except he'd got some of the Home Guard lost in the Kaimais last weekend.

'You're well tucked away here,' said Tim, as it got dark, and Graham hung a hurricane lantern from the roof of the verandah. A kerosene lamp lit the inside of the bach. 'The whole Bay's blacked out now. Everybody's driving around with their lights dimmed and banging into each other. Old Ken Craig ran into a cow the other night and flattened the front of his car.'

'Did he kill the cow?' I asked.

'No. It got up, knocked over Ken Craig, and galloped into the dark!'

'Do you think we should hide our light?' asked Mum.

'Who's going to see?' Tim laughed. 'The Japs won't, and there's no snoopers out here to report you. I reckon you're in the right place.

'Ken Craig's the E.P.S. warden, and you can't light a fag at night without him shouting and blowing his whistle. Some of the boys left an old lantern burning outside his house all one night last week. He was furious, but he couldn't do anything about it.

'You look what it says in the *Herald* about the black-out. The wharves are lit up like bonfires in Auckland, because they're working the ships all night, yet people have to black out their houses!' He laughed.

'That's what Dad says too,' said Graham.

'It gets so stuffy with everything closed,' Mum said. 'There was something about it in the *Woman's Weekly*, how depressing it makes everything. Mrs Bell at the post office said they should be prosecuted for undermining the war effort. I agree with them though. There's been no need for a black-out yet.'

'Well, it might come to it,' said Tim. 'It sounds as if the Japs are on their way to Singapore. Since they sank the *Repulse* and the *Prince of Wales*, there's nothing much to stop them.'

'What'll happen then?' Jill asked.

'I don't know.' Tim shrugged and laughed. 'Singapore's supposed to be heavily defended, but we had a talk from an officer who said they'll try to overrun Malaya, Burma, and then India. He said they could come down and attack us, and Aussie, of course.'

'I don't think we need to worry too much,' Mum said comfortably. 'It hasn't happened yet, and it probably never will.' I knew she was saying it for us, and warning Tim not to scare us. Her voice was a bit higher than usual.

'We've stepped up our patrols,' said Tim. 'They caught a spy in the Bay the other day.'

'A spy!' Jill sat forward.

'Some young chap came across on the ferry. He had a pea rifle and was a bit vague about where he was going. Ted Virtue's on holiday, so there's a replacement cop at the station. He searched the young chap's pack and found a map of the Bay.'

'He's not a spy,' I said. 'I met him in Lost Bay. His name's Simon, and he was going to join up.' Ann was the only one I'd told. Everybody else looked at me.

'George's right,' said Tim. 'It was young Simon Wheeler, from out the Mangrove River. And the cop ran him in as a spy!'

'Do you mean the Wheelers . . . ?'

'Yes,' Tim told Mum. 'One of them. Odd, isn't it! Anyway, he got on the service car to the Thames next morning, after they let him out of clink.'

'Anyone could draw a map,' said Aunty Iris.

'He reckoned he'd drawn it to remind him of the Bay,' said Tim.

We woke next morning to find Tim had gone. 'Fancy us letting him go without something to eat,' Mum said. 'He's got all that way to go, and nothing inside him.'

'He's young,' said Aunty Iris. 'I suppose he was going to meet his mates at the ferry. They keep some horses on this side.'

'What if he didn't?' said Mum. 'What if he had to cross and couldn't wake old Henry. You know what he's like in the morning after a night in the pub.'

'Then Tim would probably row himself across and leave the ferry on the other side,' said Aunty Iris. 'And old Henry will wake up and think he must have swum home from the pub last night!' They both giggled at the thought while we all watched them.

Jill called a meeting in the fort that afternoon. She wanted to talk about the Japanese.

'Fancy letting that spy go — with a map on him!' she said.

'His name was Simon — '

'Shut up! He could still have been a spy. From what I've heard, those Wheelers are a funny bunch.

'Maybe we should keep an eye on them at night, from the fort, in case they're signalling to the Japs. They could do it easily, and nobody in the Bay would know.'

I said, 'He was joining up. He was going to put up his age.'

'From now on,' Jill said, ignoring me, 'we'll keep a lookout for spies and submarines. Graham and I will patrol Lost Bay and the shack for signs. Derek, you and Jimmy can check the mouth of the creek each morning. Ann and George, you'll check the fort and patrol Whalers Beach.'

CHAPTER SEVEN
Mangrove River

'WE COULD GO TO THE Mangrove River,' said Aunty Iris.

'It would be nice to see old Mrs Cross again,' Mum said. 'But what about the Wheelers?'

'We don't have to go near them,' said Aunty Iris. 'We'll camp this side of the river, and they won't even know we've been there.'

'I'm not sailing,' said Mum.

'I'll sail.'

'Oh, can I go with Aunty Iris?' everybody said. 'Please, Mum! Please, Aunty Iris? Please, Aunty May?' But Ann and I looked at each other and knew Jill and Graham would sail with Aunty Iris because they were the eldest.

We started when it was still dark because Mum wanted to get as far as possible before the sun came up. The creek was cold as we splashed across it with Jimmy and Derek grumbling. They were only half awake. Ann and I wore pīkaus on our backs, and Mum carried a kit. The sand-hills crept out of the dark on our right, and we chased waves from the invisible sea on our left.

'Save your breath,' said Mum. 'You'll need it before we get there.' It was good, walking in a tight huddle through the dark.

By light, we could see the pōhutukawa tree that was halfway to the Mangrove River. We'd been walking backwards, trying to see the others, but nobody had seen the boat leave the creek.

At the pohutukawa, we boiled the billy, and Mum pulled out a whole lot of sandwiches. We were behind a sand-hill where the wind couldn't reach us, but the rising sun could. It wasn't as warm as the fire though.

'We'll soon be wishing it would go down again,' Mum said.

We put on our sunhats. Jimmy was running along the side of a sand-hill, when his sharp eyes spotted the others.

'Look!'

'They must have gone well out,' Mum said.

'Why?'

'There's more wind out there, and it'll be steadier.'

We ran and waved. They came about and began a long reach towards the end of the beach. We could see where the river mouth was, a low break at the end of the sand-hills.

Mum kept picking up shells, stones, bits of kauri gum, turning over seaweed, and looking at driftwood. We traced long lines behind us with sticks. It was getting hotter all the time.

I thought I could see the sails up the river, but Jimmy said it wasn't them. We staggered on. Mum said, 'George, don't run. You'll only tire yourself out.'

We trudged on across the desert. Derek walked with his tongue hanging out, till Ann said it'd get sunburnt. Then Jimmy spotted the sails moving out of the river. 'They're coming back for us!' he said.

The dinghy dipped along like a bird riding outside the breakers. We staggered to meet it, fell, crawled, and staggered on.

'We're saved!' Ann croaked. 'Here comes a camel full of water,' and we all croaked and made parched noises till our throats hurt.

Aunty Iris was on her own. She slid in, pulling up the centreboard and rudder, and letting the jib sheet fly. 'Quick!' she said. 'I can take the lot of you.'

Ann and I swung the bow around before the next wave could hit the stern and slop over it. The others piled in. The mainsail filled, and we flung ourselves in and pushed off all at once, getting wet through as a big wave lifted the bow and broke around us, but we were sailing.

Ann tightened the jib sheet, and I dropped the centreboard. Another wave lifted us, but we were over it and sailing down its back.

'Whee!' we all yelled, but Mum just held on tight.

'Better than dying of thirst!' Ann said, and we grinned at each other. The sun was so hot now, our wet clothes didn't matter.

As we ran in over the bar, Aunty Iris said, 'We saw a couple of sharks on our way in: reremai. They often lie in the shallows here.'

'Look!' Jimmy yelled. Scared by our shadow, a sting-ray skimmed like a dark thought over the lip of the bar and disappeared into the deeper water inside. Upstream, smoke lifted where Jill and Graham boiled the billy.

It was like landing in another country. We ran up, and they told us about the sharks.

'It's not fair,' Jimmy said. 'You see everything, just because you're the biggest.'

After lunch, Mum decided we'd visit Mrs Cross before putting up the camp, so we rowed over the river, pulled the dinghy up, and climbed around the rocks.

'She must be as old as the hills now,' Mum said. 'She seemed old enough when I was your age.

'They all used to sail into the Bay in their whaleboat, load up with stores, and head home, and we wouldn't see them for another three months. Her husband worked in the kauri, and she'd followed him from job to job, bringing up a string of kids in nīkau whares and ponga huts. He drowned on the bar across the mouth of the river, the kids grew up and wandered away, and she just stayed on out here by herself, getting older and older.

'Now, you watch your manners when you meet her. She's very cross-eyed, so don't you go staring at her. Jimmy, don't you dare cross your eyes while we're there!'

It was just as well Mum had warned us. Old Mrs Cross came to her door looking like the witch in the gingerbread house. She was so wrinkled she looked tattooed. Her hands were knots. She wore a dress down to the ground, with a sack apron over it, and her back was so bent, she had to lift her head to look at us. Strangest of all, when Mum called her name, she looked in the other direction.

'May Millen!' she said, 'and Iris! I'd know those voices anywhere.' She kissed them, but looked at us while she was doing so. Mum told her our names, and she shook hands with us, mumbling our names over and over, running them into one long word. She had the oldest voice I'd heard. She had no teeth. Best of all, she was so cross-eyed, she looked away while she talked to us. We were fascinated!

Her cottage had two rooms, one filled with a brass bedstead. The other was her living-room, and it wasn't big enough for all of us. One end was a chimney, like a room on its own. Though it was a hot day, a fire burned in it between the seats that ran either side, inside the chimney itself.

'You won't see another chimney like that!' old Mrs Cross chuckled, her chin working up and down. I realized she was talking to me, though she was looking at Ann.

'Go on, try it!' she said, and we walked into it and sat down, three each side.

'Ingle-benches!' old Mrs Cross mumbled, and we slipped outside, while she was busy talking to Mum and Aunty Iris.

'Boy,' said Derek, 'that fire was hot!'

'That's where she roasted Hansel and Gretel,' said Ann.

'Did she really? Is she a witch?'

'No! She's just very old.'

Jill groaned. 'They're going to have a cup of tea. That means we'll be here for hours.'

Mum came to the door. 'Mrs Cross says you can help yourselves to plums,' she said. 'The orchard's up the back.'

The fruit trees were surrounded by a dark hedge covered with red and white roses. Many had fallen, but several plum trees dripped ripe fruit. We gorged on yellow ones, juice running down our chins. The peaches were too green, even for Graham who could eat them hard.

Old Mrs Cross gave each of us a piece of fruit cake, very dark and heavy, when we left. 'Come back and see me,' she said 'and I'll tell you about the Bay in the old days, things your mother and aunt don't remember because they were too young.'

She shook hands again and hugged Ann. 'You're just

like your mother,' she said, looking away to one side of her. 'Such a pretty girl she was. Her name was Ann too.'

We ran down the grassy slope between the pōhutukawas and on to the beach, as if escaping. When I looked back, she was calling goodbye and looking the wrong way.

'I could live here!' I said, looking at the little bay with its beach, its trees, and its cottage.

'Not much good if the Japs came,' said Jill.

As we went back, Jimmy and Derek tried talking to each other and looking the other way. I tried crossing my eyes, but couldn't look away as she did.

'Can we go back and see her again?' I asked Mum, and she thought I was being rude, but I liked old Mrs Cross and her cottage with the ingle-benches inside the chimney.

Among the pōhutukawas across the river, Aunty Iris and Graham stretched a rope between two branches, and we threw a huge fly over it, making a tent big enough for us all. While Jill and Graham got pipis from the river, we dragged driftwood to the camp and cooked the pipis in a kerosene tin over the fire. Aunty Iris tipped them out on a plank, and we sat around it and ate pipis with bread and butter. The shells were hot, the juice burned our fingers, and they were sweet.

'I like Mum's bread,' said Jimmy, 'but I miss the kissing bread off the loaves at home.'

'Kissing crust!' said Derek.

'Same thing,' said Mum. 'Different names, that's all. I'll bake some separate loaves, and you can have all the kissing bread you want.'

'Can you make it in the camp oven?'

'Of course. Come on, clear these shells away.'

Where others had thrown their shells, we threw ours too. There'd been so many feasts of pipis there, a whole bank of shells had grown. The wind had cut through the sand-hill at one place and had revealed shells so old they were softish and black. There was charcoal amongst them.

'People have sat here and eaten pipis for hundreds and hundreds of years,' said Aunty Iris.

We rolled ourselves in our blankets. Mum and Aunty Iris sat by the fire, and Aunty Iris must have smoked, because I could smell her tobacco. Their voices wound through the steady beat of the waves on the bar.

CHAPTER EIGHT
What's a Conchy?

UP THE RIVER NEXT MORNING a puff of smoke appeared and vanished, as if somebody had waved a white flag once.

'That's the hermit,' said Aunty Iris. 'He's been living on Mangrove Island since the year dot.'

'Alone?'

'Yes.' She stood and looked again, but there was nothing more. 'He probably lit his fire with kauri kindling. That's what would have smoked. Now, he'll have it going with mangrove. Good firewood, mangrove. It burns for ages.

'Remember,' she said, 'when he chased us?'

'Yes.' Mum laughed. 'Remember his dog? We thought it was going to get us. Your mother was with us,' she said to Ann.

'What happened? Oh, tell us, Aunty May!'

We'd finished breakfast and were sitting around. Mum smiled at Ann. 'Nothing much happened,' she said.

'We'd sailed from the bach to visit Mrs Cross, one summer years before any of you were even thought of. Father said the bar was dangerous, and we weren't to come inside the river. Father would have been furious if he'd known.

'We sailed up the river and landed on Mangrove Island. It was Ann's idea to look for the hermit. She was always getting the rest of us into trouble. She disappeared ahead of us into the mangroves, and we heard the most terrible baying. Iris and I hung on to each other and shrieked — yes you did, Iris! — and Ann came racing out of the mangroves, grabbed us, and the three of us fell over together into the black mud. We were all in long frocks. Fancy going sailing today in long frocks!

'The tide was going out, and we had to shove the boat

off. We were filthy with black mud and wet through, crying and laughing at once.'

They were doing it again, Aunty Iris and Mum, laughing and crying all at once, and we all started laughing too, though we didn't know why.

'Go on,' said Ann.

'We pulled up the sail,' Mum said, 'and the gaff fell and hit Ann on the head!' She had to stop talking, she was laughing so much.

'Go on!' we all shrieked at her.

'We got it up, all lopsided, and pushed off, as the hermit and a huge dog came running out of the mangroves. He was jumping up and down and shouting, and his dog jumped up and down and barked too.

'And Ann started jumping up and down and barking back at them!'

'Stop it!' said Aunty Iris. She was rocking, tears running down her face.

'Then Ann jumped too high!' shrieked Mum. 'She jumped so high, she jumped out of the boat!'

We all howled and rolled about the camp. 'What happened? What happened?'

'We dragged her aboard, the wind picked up, and we sailed away, just as the dog came swimming and barking after us.'

'Would it have bitten you?'

'Perhaps not. Maybe they were just lonely. We shouldn't have been there, and that made it worse.'

'What'd you do?'

'We sailed around to Mrs Cross's, and she helped us rinse our clothes. We sat in her big chimney and dried them, before we sailed home.

'We had to tell Mother, because she knew at once we'd been up to something, but Father — your grandfather — never found out.'

'And my mother fell out of the boat?' asked Ann.

'Yes,' said Mum. 'She was so busy jumping up and down and barking at the dog, she went right over the side. I can still see her frock spread out around her like a big white flower as she went under. Oh, dear!' and Mum wiped her eyes.

'Is it the same hermit?' asked Jill.

'Yes, he must be as old as Mrs Cross.'

'What'll happen to him if the Japs come?'

'Don't be silly. The Japs aren't coming.

'The Wheelers keep an eye on him, from time to time. One of them goes across to Mrs Cross every day. They're very kind to her, she said yesterday.'

'Is that their place up there?'

'Yes. They keep to themselves. It must be a funny sort of life.'

The Wheelers lived across the river, a mile or so up. There was something funny about them, we knew without being told. They only came into the Bay occasionally, picked up their stores, and went home without talking to anybody much at all.

They always had a couple of bags of mail to post, and they got lots of mail from all around the world, everybody knew that.

The four boys had all belonged to the Correspondence School, and then they'd gone to boarding school up in Auckland, come home, and worked on the farm.

The farm ran away up into the hills above the Mangrove River. There was no road, so their wool went out on a big scow which came in on the high tide, loaded, and skimmed out on top of the next one. If they missed the spring tide, the scow could get stuck inside the bar for weeks.

We swam, while Aunty Iris, Jill, and Graham caught snapper in the channel. Aunty Iris gutted and split them open, leaving the scales on, and hung them above the fire. 'Keep it smoking with tea-tree', she said, 'and it'll give them a bit of flavour.'

Derek was sunburnt so he had to keep in the shade. We left him to smoke the fish with Jimmy, and the rest of us rowed across to get some oysters off the rocks.

The others used hammers and screwdrivers to flick off the shells, and scooped the oysters into Agee jars. Ann and I knocked a few open with stones, and licked them out of their shells, working our way around the point and out of sight.

We climbed through the trees and followed sheep tracks along the hill, looking down through the pōhutukawa branches at the water, and reached a clear spur. The Mangrove River spread for miles beneath us, a vast sheet of water with long arms disappearing between hills. The hermit's was only one of thousands of mangrove islands. A mangrove forest spread along both sides of the river; islands, swamps, sand-bars all covered with mangroves. Everywhere, channels wound between them, disappeared, and showed again, silver streaks amongst the dull, green trees.

'I didn't know it was so big,' said Ann.

'Mum said there were more farms up there in the old days, and the scow used to go away up to them, but they all went back into bush.'

'Why?'

'The scows stopped coming. I don't know why. I suppose the bar got shallower or something.'

'Hallo!' a strange voice said, and we both jumped with fright, but it was a kind-looking woman who said, smiling at us, 'I'm Mrs Wheeler. You must be May Millen's children.'

'I'm George,' I said. 'This is Ann, my cousin.'

'Then Ann was your mother?'

'Yes.'

'Your mother and I grew up together,' said Mrs Wheeler. 'We went to school together in the Bay. She was my best friend.

'I've just been over to see Mrs Cross. She told me you'd been to see her. Come down to the house.'

It was just around the shoulder of the hill, built on a grassy flat, and surrounded with trees and flowers. We could see an orchard and a big vegetable garden. There were beehives beside a hedge. A dog barked from under a tree, and Mrs Wheeler told him to be quiet.

Past the house, a jetty ran out through the mangroves, and a white launch was tied there.

We crunched along a shell path past roses and tottering rods of hollyhocks, in a door, and down a step into a wide kitchen. The sun fell on the floor through open windows. There was a fireplace at one end, with armchairs and a couch around it. Chairs stood around a long table. A big stove was at the other end.

'Harry and the boys are mustering,' said Mrs Wheeler. 'Try some lemonade?'

It was sweet and bitter all at once, with lumps of lemon floating in it. We sat in the cool kitchen, ate biscuits and cake, and talked about the Bay. Mrs Wheeler kept looking at Ann, and I could see she reminded her of Aunty Ann, whom none of us could remember.

She'd heard Dad was missing, but didn't know he was a prisoner of war.

'Do you think the Japs are coming?' I asked her.

'They might,' she said, 'but I really don't think so. We're a very long way from Japan.'

I wondered if I should tell her about meeting Simon, but she didn't seem to want to talk about the war. When I told her about Jill's patrols, she just smiled.

We liked sitting in the comfortable kitchen. I could see Ann and Mrs Wheeler liked each other. When we left, she gave us a big billy of milk and a basket of scones. 'Just leave the billy and basket on the end of the jetty when you're going past,' she said.

She looked sad and kissed Ann. As we climbed the track, we looked back, and she was watching still. She waved, and we waved back.

Mum and Aunty Iris were strange when we told them where we'd been.

'Phyllis Wheeler!' Mum said. 'Shouldn't we go and see her, since she knows we're here?'

'How can we?' Aunty Iris said. 'They're conchies.'

'That's not her fault.'

'Still, we can't, and you know why. Writing letters against the war, and keeping their sons at home . . . They're just hiding behind the men who've gone.'

'Tim said one's joined up.'

'Yes, but he had to run away to do it. Look at Stan: wounded and a prisoner of war. And look at what's happened to Rod. And there's all those other boys who won't come back. And they're safe here. Does that seem right to you?'

It was as close as I'd heard them come to arguing. Mum looked like crying.

'Mrs Wheeler doesn't think the Japs are coming,' I said.

'Oh, she doesn't! I wonder how she knows?' said Aunty Iris. 'Perhaps she'd like to keep her ideas to herself.'

She and Graham rowed in silence. Jill was in the bow. Ann and I were in the stern with Mum.

'What's a conchy?' I asked Mum, but she didn't answer.

'A conchy's a coward who won't fight for his country,' said Aunty Iris. 'Conscientious objectors, they're called. They won't fight, but they let others fight for them.'

We were going up the river, instead of across, heading for the Wheelers' jetty. Graham followed Aunty Iris's rowing. Jill hung on to a pile, and Aunty Iris leaned out and put the untouched billy of milk and basket of scones on the end of the jetty. I hoped Mrs Wheeler wasn't watching.

Aunty Iris said, 'Decent people won't take anything from conchies!'

'What about Mrs Cross?' I asked.

'That's different!'

Nobody said anything more. We crossed to our camp. Ann was leaning hard against me, and I could feel her crying. I saw her look back to the billy and the basket, and I saw Mum look back too.

CHAPTER NINE
Fried Scones

JIMMY AND DEREK KNEW SOMETHING was wrong and didn't say much. We ate some of the smoked snapper for tea and went straight to bed. Mum and Aunty Iris didn't sit up by the fire.

I looked across in the darkness and wondered if the billy and basket were still at the end of the jetty. When I heard Ann sniffing, I reached and patted her, and she hung on to my hand.

We had porridge in the dark and were off back to the bach before dawn.

'It's going to swing around and come in from the north-east,' Aunty Iris said. I couldn't tell which way the wind was coming, in fact, where we were there wasn't any wind at all, but she knew about things like that.

'At bit of extra ballast won't hurt,' she said. 'I'll take Ann and George as well. We'll be running ahead of it most of the way.'

Mum made us put on extra pullovers. We could hardly climb into the boat. Ann and Graham rowed with an oar each. Jill was in the stern with Aunty Iris. The currrent swept us downriver, and we scraped the bar once but carried clear.

'There's the nor-easter beginning,' Aunty Iris said, and I felt air move on my cheek. We slid the oars under the thwarts, and Jill started shouting orders at us.

'There's only one skipper on a boat, Jill,' said Aunty Iris.

Graham dropped the centreboard. He and Ann pulled on the halyard, and the mainsail swayed up under its spar in the dark. Jill tightened the sheet, and Aunty Iris turned the nose of the boat, so she picked up the wind. A ripply noise came from under the bow.

'All right, George!' I pulled up the jib and cleated the

halyard. Graham pulled in the sheet, and the boat came alive under us.

We reached across towards the islands. It was too dark to see the beach, and the sea was too rough anyway. I wondered if you could run into the islands in the dark, or if they'd show up.

'It's all right,' Aunty Iris called. 'We'll gybe soon and run for the creek. It's smoother going downhill.' Spray came back over us, and there was a thump beneath my feet.

Dawn came quickly. It touched with red the islands, the tips of the waves, some clouds along the horizon, and the sails. Even our faces looked red. Spray flew back and, now and then, the top of a wave slopped over the side. Aunty Iris ignored it, but, when there was enough in the bottom, Graham bailed it.

Well out, Jill pulled in the mainsheet until the boom was almost in the middle of the boat, and Aunty Iris shifted the tiller until we were moving off before the wind, instead of reaching across it. Jill let out the sheet, and the mainsail swung right out over the waves. Suddenly, it was smooth sailing.

'Keep the jib out on the other side,' Aunty Iris said. 'She'll run wing and wing.'

'Wing and wong!' I could hear Ann clearly over the wind in the rigging, the splashing under the bows, the creaking of the boom and gaff jaws on the mast.

'Try coming back, George,' said Aunty Iris, 'beside Ann.'

I slid back over the thwart and crouched beside her. The bow rose a little, and we slid down the back of a wave. Aunty Iris sat forward, her hand light on the tiller. As we coasted down a wave, she turned it ever so slightly, and the sail drew us on, as the great animal of water beneath passed on, and another took its place.

From the tops of the waves, I could see the beach, but we were too far out to see anybody. I glanced back as a huge wave rose above Aunty Iris's shoulder. I was going to yell, but our stern lifted, we rode forward and dropped behind it, and another followed, just as big.

Aunty Iris grinned. 'Doesn't pay to look back,' she called.

A gannet came down the sky, skidded along the face of a wave, circled us, lifted, and was gone. Aunty Iris nodded, and there were some Mother Carey's chickens dodging in and out of sight between the waves.

So, we ran all the way into the creek. Later, Graham said he'd have put a reef in the main, but Aunty Iris knew how to sail. 'She's very safe,' he said, 'but she does like to sail fast.'

Off the creek, I went forward and dropped the jib, and Graham lifted the centreboard, as a wave lifted us, carried us between the knife-edged walls of sand at the mouth, and swept us into the creek.

We floated in still water out of the wind. The waves thumped on Whalers Beach in growing surf, but we ghosted around the bend where the pōhutukawa leaned above its reflection, and its stamens floated like blood on the new tide.

'Good run!' was all Aunty Iris said, but I knew she was pleased. There was colour in her face, and she took out her tobacco pouch and rolled herself a cigarette, as we drifted in beside the steps, lowered the sail, and began unloading.

We lit the fire and brought down several loads of wood. Aunty Iris said we were in for some dirty weather. When we'd got everything in place, Ann and I took the dinghy across the creek and ran back to meet Mum, Jimmy, and Derek.

At first they were just a dot along Whalers Beach, then three dots, then we could see them moving, and last we could see they were people. We ran with our mouths open, so our cheeks filled with wind. It was almost blowing us backwards now.

Breakers rode in, curled, dragging wings of spray, and boomed down. Every now and then, a really big one would collapse and sweep right up the beach and around our feet. We were too scared to run up and down between the monsters. The water swirled up and sucked the sand under our feet. We felt it trying to drag us out.

The others came towards us quickly. 'You must have had a fast sail,' Mum said.

'Corker!' I told her. 'We blew right into the creek.'

It was much easier walking back. The sand and spray whipped the backs of our legs, but not our faces. We spread our arms and blew like sails, skittered up into the sand-hills, leapt down on the beach, and kicked our way through the froth that was building up.

Rain was spitting, as we reached the dinghy. Aunty Iris and Jill helped us tie up beside the steps, as hard drops pelted the creek before a new sort of wind, one which swept around the bend and lifted spray off the creek. Heavy rain ripped the water like those machine-gun bullets we'd all seen on the newsreels at the pictures. But the wind didn't reach the bach itself, it was so well tucked away under the cliff and the pōhutukawa.

'It sounds like big guns on the beach,' Mum said.

'It's come up quickly,' Aunty Iris said. 'You got back just in time.'

'And not one of us wet,' said Mum. 'I'm dying for a cuppa!'

'Sit yourself down. There's one just made.' Jill was filling our mugs from the billy, and there were smoking-hot scones with lumps of butter melting into them. I looked at Ann and thought it was Aunty Iris's way of saying she was sorry about Mrs Wheeler's scones and milk.

She rolled herself a cigarette. The fire crackled, as Graham threw on a piece of driftwood that caught and flared green and blue.

'It's a good day to be home safe in the bach,' Mum said, and then somebody remembered it was Christmas Eve, and we sat up late and listened to the storm.

Mum said, 'I hope nobody's out in this,' and I wondered if she was thinking about Dad.

'One thing, the Japs won't come tonight,' said Graham.

'It's just the night they would come,' said Jill, 'when everyone's inside, thinking they're safe.'

'Well, I wouldn't like to try landing tonight,' said Aunty Iris. 'Those waves are coming right up the creek.'

It was roaring more than ever the next morning when I woke and opened the parcel by my pillow. It was a book, as I'd hoped, a big green book called *Westward Ho!* by Charles Kingsley. Ann wasn't awake, so I read the first page, and it wasn't much, and there was another paragraph, over the page, then a white space, and then the proper story began:

One bright summer's afternoon, in the year of grace 1575, a tall and fair boy came lingering along Bideford Quay in his scholar's gown, with satchel and slate in hand, watching wistfully the shipping and the sailors . . .

I snuggled down in my bunk, Ann's head just behind mine. The storm roared, the ocean slammed on Whalers Beach, but I heard only the words of John Oxenham and gaped at the King of Mexico's Quezal bird.

'I said, "What've you got?"' Ann hissed in my ear. 'George, I've been talking to you for ages, and you haven't heard a word.' I showed her my book and looked at hers: *Anne of Green Gables*.

'It's got an e.'

'I know. It's all right.'

'Can I read it after you?'

'Mmm.'

A few minutes later, she turned over and whispered, 'I know this Mrs Rachel Lynde in my book. She's Mrs Montague across the street at home. She sits in her window, sewing and knitting, and watches everything I do. She's always telling Dad how he should bring up a daughter.'

She laughed, and I grinned. Uncle Paul always said it'd be easier to have three boys, and he tried to get Ann to wear the same clothes and to do the same things as Graham and Derek. She said she didn't mind. She got her own way, she said.

The others stirred, looked at their presents, asked everybody else what they'd got, and it was quiet again, everybody lying reading. The storm blew outside, and nobody wanted to get up. Mum and Aunty Iris were still asleep.

Then a voice muttered, 'Cup of tea.' There was silence, and it groaned and moaned, 'Cup of tea?' in a winning way. Aunty Iris was waking up.

There was a long silence. Ann turned a page and giggled. I bent my head around so I could see her. I liked watching Ann read. She always laughed and cried, so you could tell what was happening in a story just by watching her. Sometimes, though, I made her read to me, because I couldn't bear not hearing the words.

'It's Christmas for me too,' said Aunty Iris, 'but nobody's brought me a cup of tea.'

We all lay very still.

'Nobody thinks of me at Christmas,' she said. 'Nobody loves me.'

Another silence.

'Oh well,' she said, 'I suppose I'll have to leap out and light the fire and make a cup of tea,' but she didn't move, nor did any of us. We knew her tricks.

'You stay in your beds, warm and comfortable,' she tried again. 'You're young, and you've got the whole of your lives ahead of you. I'm old, and my life's nearly over, so I'll leap up and light the fire and go out into the storm to get wood and water, and I'll make the tea and cook the breakfast even though it's Christmas, because I'm old and I don't matter and nobody loves me and — '

'Oh, all right!' Jill shouted. She jumped out of her bunk, ran across and stuffed dry tea-tree into the fireplace. 'I'll make a cup of tea, just to stop you moaning.'

'Merry Christmas!' shouted Aunty Iris.

'Merry Christmas!' we all shouted and went on reading.

'It's Christmas,' said Aunty Iris. Jill banged wood on the fire, banged the billy on its hook, and banged her way out of the door.

'It's Christmas, and nobody wants to talk to me. All over the world, it's Christmas, and people are talking to each other, but nobody talks to me.'

'I'm reading,' I said.

'That's nice for you, George,' said Aunty Iris. 'What are you reading?'

'Shhh!' Ann clamped her hand over my mouth.

'What did you say you're reading?'

A big giggle was coming up inside me. I was going to splutter. Ann pushed her hand down. 'Shhh!'

'I'm lonely,' said Aunty Iris. 'It's Christmas, and nobody wants to talk to me.' We lay still. 'I might as well go out into the storm by myself and gather firewood, like poor old Good King Wenceslas.'

'Oh, drat you!' Mum said. 'You've woken us all now. Come on, we'll go for a run in the storm.'

We threw on our clothes, ran down the creek, and bolted across near the mouth. Froth was waist-deep against the sand-hills. Logs were dumped on the sand. We ran and shrieked in the wind, leaned into it off the sand-hills till we fell and rolled down. Aunty Iris and Mum made more noise than the rest of us. The wind whipped the cries out of our mouths. Then we turned and ran for the bach, wet and cold, splashing across the creek, through froth, bits of pumice, and mangrove berries.

We drank tea and had fried scones for breakfast, big, golden, fried scones, fried in the camp oven. We stood on the verandah, the storm tossed spray over the sand-hills, and we ate fried scones with golden syrup, tossing them from hand to hand because they were so hot.

In a hundred years, if you ask any of us about the bach and what we remember best, I'll bet we'd all say, 'Fried scones!'

And that was Christmas Day. Later, we saw dead seagulls float up the creek, and the snake-headed body of a black shag.

I remember standing in the fort, the wind trying to take off our heads as we lifted them above the parapet, watching the line of breakers parading in to collapse and smash on the beach. They shook us. The air was too full of spray and spume for us to see towards the Mangrove River, but I wondered about the Wheelers.

Ann said they'd be sitting in front of their fire, eating

fried scones. 'Mrs Cross'll be sitting inside her chimney, eating fried scones,' she said, 'and the hermit will be sitting in front of his fire with his feet resting on his dog, and they'll both be eating fried scones.'

Jill said the Wheelers would go and see Mrs Cross was all right.

'They're kind to her,' said Ann.

'They're still conchies!' snapped Jill. 'I don't know about the hermit though. His island must be nearly under water.'

'Does his hut get flooded?' I asked.

For a moment, I thought Jill was going to speak as if she'd been there, as if she knew his island well. I held my breath, but she remembered just in time: Girl Guides never lie. 'I don't know,' she said. 'I've never been there.'

'Luke Kelly says he's seen it flooded,' said Graham. 'He said the hermit told him he's had crocodiles snapping all around his bed, when the river came inside his hut.'

'Is that true?' asked Jimmy.

'Luke Kelly says so. He says that's why the hermit's bed has got very long legs; he has to jump to get into it.'

'Aw!'

'He'll be all right. His island's built up with shells and logs. It's quite high, Aunty Iris said. And he's got a big punt. He could always row down to the Wheelers.'

'I wonder if he does eat fried scones,' I said.

'Doesn't everybody?' Derek asked.

'Race you home!' said Jimmy, 'and we'll ask Mum to make some more.'

We leapt into the jumping pit. The wet sand didn't slide. We ran across the sand-hills and saw smoke rising from the bach. Mum was hanging our wet things on the verandah. It looked safe out of the storm.

CHAPTER TEN
The Scow

JILL WANTED TO START THE patrols again, but we weren't interested, besides, the storm went on for days. Ann woke me one morning, and there was still a great shout from the sea, but the wind had dropped. I could feel the warmth from the fireplace, even though the fire was out, as we stole past.

'There might be some kauri gum on the beach,' said Ann, as we cut through the sand-hills to the fort. We climbed the wall, leaned beside a driftwood gun, and looked out to sea.

The sun was fighting its way through a yellow murk, where breakers still tottered and collapsed. Below, driven hard against the bottom of the fort, a wrecked scow lay.

I shouted something to Ann, but my voice disappeared in the sea's boom.

The sea had drawn back. The scow looked like a wounded animal that had crawled up to escape the ravening surf and died. She was smashed badly. Half-way along one side, there was a funny angle, as if she'd been bent. The fallen mast hid a lot of damage. The other side had planks ripped off, ribs open to the sea. Any cargo must have washed out. We walked inside her, swung ourselves up, and stood on what was left of her deck. Ropes and seaweed were everywhere. Sand half-filled her.

'I wonder what happened to her crew?' I said.

'Perhaps the Japs got them,' said Ann.

'There's no sign of anybody.'

'We'd better tell Aunty Iris and Aunty May.'

As we came in sight of the bach, we shouted, 'A wreck! Quick! A wreck!'

Jill and Graham dressed and vanished. Mum lit the fire and said she'd get something cooking, and Aunty Iris ran with the rest of us, pointing, shouting, grabbing each other, and staring at the fabulous wreck.

Graham and Jill were already on the deck by the stump of the mast. Aunty Iris had a quick look round and said, 'We'd better hunt through the sand-hills, just in case somebody's alive.'

While they spread and searched, Ann and I went up the beach towards the half-way tree. There were planks and boxes, and what looked like a shed that must have been torn off the deck. We found a torn piece of sail, but nothing else, just the usual logs, pumice, and a few bits of kauri gum we picked up. There was nobody in the sand-hills either.

'Was she torpedoed?' Jill asked Aunty Iris.

'Goodness, no! She probably ran on one of the islands and was carried in here.'

'What about the crew?'

'Drowned, I'm afraid. They couldn't have lived in that sea.'

'How many?'

'Two or three. She looks like the old *Miriam K* to me. Luke Kelly's son, Pat, was on her, but joined up months ago. Teddy Ray and Tom Whiting were going to join up too. I don't know who'd be sailing her now.'

Mum arrived and said, 'If there's no survivors we'd all better have something hot to eat.'

Jill talked of what we'd do with the wreck, how we'd make it part of the fort.

'Don't forget Ann and I found it first,' I said. 'It's ours.'

'Don't forget it still belongs to somebody else,' said Jill.

Mum had made a thick soup, a sort of fish stew of mussels and flounder with chopped-up onions and potatoes. We ate it out of mugs. I drank mine and ate the solid part with a spoon.

'It could have been a mine,' said Aunty Iris. 'There have been stories of them breaking loose and floating around.'

'Like the one that got the *Niagara*?' said Graham.

'Maybe.'

'But the Japs weren't in the war then?'

'No, that one was laid by a German raider.'

'What's a raider?' asked Jimmy.

'A fast ship that lays mines, and shells everything it can. They're often disguised as merchant ships.'

'I wonder if the Japs have them?'

After breakfast, Aunty Iris and Jill set off to walk into the Bay and report the wreck. We spent the day playing on it.

By next morning the sea had gone down. We were rolling logs down the beach and floating them up the creek to the bach for firewood, when Constable Virtue rode his horse along the beach. He must have followed another track somewhere, because he couldn't get a horse down ours.

Aunty Iris and Jill got back later and said he'd crossed the Bay river with them, swimming his horse behind the ferry.

He searched the wreck and the sand-hills and came to the bach for lunch. He asked Ann and me about finding the wreck and if we'd taken anything from it. Aunty Iris had thrown a lot of rope under the bach, but we didn't tell him about that. He said he'd search the length of Whalers Beach and check with the Wheelers.

'Not that I'd rely on a bunch of conchies,' he said. 'They'll have to watch themselves, that lot.'

'Ted Virtue!' Mum said. 'Phyllis went to school with us. She's a McLeod!'

'All the same. . . ' said Constable Virtue. 'Their youngest boy came into the Bay before Christmas and went over to the Thames to join up. Must be made of better stuff than the rest.'

He said nothing about Simon being arrested for a spy.

'How's the news?' Mum asked him.

'War's going splendidly,' he said, but when she asked about the Japanese, he didn't seem to know much.

'One thing's for certain,' he said. 'They'll never get past Singapore. Impregnable!' he said. 'Impregnable!'

Ann looked at me. I could see her saying *impregnable* silently.

When he'd ridden off, Jimmy and Derek started throwing balls of horse dung at each other. Derek ducked and Jill got hit instead as she came down the track behind Aunty Iris. She punched Jimmy, and he bellowed. Mum made us clean up the muck.

'Shovel it into the creek,' she said, 'so it floats out. I don't know why people always have to ride their horses right up to a place!'

Later, when we were playing on the wreck again, pretending it was being torpedoed, Jill came along and started on about the Japs again.

'You might think it's just a game,' she said, 'but I think she was sunk by the Japs. Aunty Iris and I listened to the news in the Bay last night, and it sounds as if they are going to attack New Zealand.'

'Aunty Iris said she probably ran on one of the islands.'

'Then why didn't she stay on it?' asked Jill. 'Have any of you looked at this?' and she pulled at the smashed ends of the planks. 'See, they look charred. It must've been an explosion to do that.

'I think the grown-ups are hiding something from us. It must've been a torpedo that sank her. I reckon the Japs did it and killed the crew. We didn't hear them because of the storm.

'Look out there. A Jap submarine could be looking at us through their periscope now . . .'

The hairs on my neck stood up. 'Let's go home,' I said.

'Not that way, you fool! If they're watching, they'll know where the bach is.'

After that we tried to come on to the beach through the sand-hills, and we always disappeared through them, so the Japs wouldn't find the bach.

Constable Virtue came back with two other men a few days later. He told us they were inspecting the wreck, but Jill said they were looking for signs of the Japs. Next day we were in the fort when we saw a string of horses come down from the sand-hills near the half-way tree. They rode towards us in a group: the Mounted Rifles. The horses looked beautiful, splashing water, tossing sand. The men dismounted and had a look at the wreck. One spotted us, pointed, and we ran home.

'They'll be on their way to the Bay,' said Aunty Iris. 'Ted Virtue said they were exercising in the hills.'

There was a great splashing, and three soldiers rode down the creek. One was Tim, and we knew the others, a farmer from the Bay, and a fisherman.

'Good-day!' Tim yelled. 'We're out scaring the Japs!' Aunty Iris waved a mug, but he called, 'Got to get back!' and they trotted down to the others.

We sat in the wreck later after looking at their tracks.

'A few men on horses aren't going to scare the Japs,' said Jill. 'They'll have tanks and guns.'

'The Mounted Rifles have guns,' said Derek. He and Jimmy wanted to join them and ride horses.

'Carbines!' said Graham.

'Pea-shooters!' said Jill. 'What good will they be against tanks?'

We were silent because she was right. The Mounted Rifles weren't going to stop the Japs, not if they were out there just waiting to land.

'How many were there?' I asked.

'About thirty,' said Graham.

Jill shook her head. 'Twenty-four. I counted them,' she said.

When I think about it now, I realize until then we had been playing with the idea that the Japs were coming. But, from that moment when Jill said she had counted the Mounted Rifles, as we sat and talked in the wreck, we were convinced by Jill that they were coming, and that nobody could do anything about it. From then on, we were just going to follow her, and everything that happened seemed unavoidable.

'The bach is hidden,' I said.

'It's the first place they'd find,' said Jill. 'They'd come straight up the creek.'

'What about up in the hills?'

'That'd be better.'

But Aunty Iris laughed, when we asked her. 'What would

you live on up in the hills?' she asked. 'And where would you live?'

'There must have been camps up there,' said Graham.

'There were — in the kauri days. There were logging camps all over the place. But they're long gone.'

'I bet Mrs Cross knows plenty,' I said.

'She would, but you'd be lucky to find any sign of them now. A few pongas here, a bit of second-growth there. That's all you'd find now.

'There were some goldminers' camps, but they're gone too.'

CHAPTER ELEVEN
A Place to Hide

WE TOOK THE DINGHY UP the creek as far as we could go, and pushed through the scrub, looking for the track the policeman and the Mounted Rifles had used. Our track climbed over the hills behind the cliffs and dropped down on Whauwhau Beach. Jill thought, if we could find the old track to the Mangrove River, we might find a place to hide in the hills.

The scrub was harder to push through than tea-tree, spiky, dry scrub with hard, brown nuts growing on it. It scratched us. Dust choked us. The sun was overhead.

'We're lost!' Jimmy said.

Immediately, we all felt we were.

'Nonsense!' Jill said in her best Girl Guide voice, and she hoisted Derek on her shoulders to see where we were.

'Can you see the track?'

'No.'

'What about the hills?'

'No.'

'Well, you must be able to see the creek.'

'I can't see anything but scrub. It goes on and on. I want to get down.'

Jill dumped him. 'I know where we are!' she shouted.

'We're lost!' Jimmy repeated.

'We're only a few chains from the creek,' said Jill. 'Look! You can see where we came!' She was right. We'd left a trail of flattened grass and broken branches.

'You hurt me,' Derek whined. 'You didn't have to drop me like that.'

'Oh, come on!' Jill pushed in front of Graham, and he followed her. The rest of us sat down, sick of the heat, the dust, the scratches from scrub and cutty grass.

'I want a drink of water,' said Jimmy.

'Come on!' Jill yelled. 'We're on the track. Come on! I've found it!'

'I don't care,' said Jimmy.

Jill came crashing back. 'I heard that,' she said. 'You'll care all right if the Japs come. We've found a way to the track from the bach, and you say you don't care.'

When we followed her, the track was bare, red clay, and we could see where horses had been along it. It disappeared into the scrub, reappeared, and disappeared again. We knew it went far enough to come down on Whalers Beach near the halfway tree, but the rest of it had disappeared like the camps, the mines, the kauri and gold, and the farms it had once served up the Mangrove River.

Just where we turned to go back, Jill found a stake with a square of white canvas. Somebody had daubed a red circle on it.

'A Jap flag!' she said.

'The Mounted Rifles must have left it,' said Graham.

'What would they be doing with a Japanese flag?'

'They were doing exercises,' he said weakly.

'With Japanese flags?' She ripped it off the stake and rolled it up. 'Come on, we're going home.'

Perhaps she was right. We followed her back through the scrub and rowed the dinghy home.

When we told Mum about finding the track, she said, 'You be careful. It's easy to get lost in the scrub. Don't let Jimmy and Derek get out of sight of the rest of you. They're only little, remember.'

Jill didn't like being told that. She wanted to do the right thing always, but never seemed able to please Mum. I understood that and it didn't annoy me. Jimmy was Mum's favourite, and nothing was going to alter that.

It was as if being a Girl Guide, never telling a lie, and all the rest of it wasn't enough, and Jill couldn't understand it. She'd keep on trying, and Mum would keep on being the same.

That afternoon we met in the fort, and Jill said we should

go further up the track, now we knew where it was, and look for other tracks branching off from it.

'When Uncle Dugald was a boy, they used to take supplies on pack-horses to camps up in the hills,' she said. 'I've heard him talk about it. There must be some old huts up there still.

'We'll make a map,' she said. 'We'll go up the track and map any others we can find. It'll be the beginning of our plan.' Jill was a great one for plans.

Mum gave us sandwiches, a billy, and stuff for making tea. We each had a pīkau with our mug and our share of the lunch.

'Just remember,' Mum said, 'keep everyone in sight all the time. You're the oldest,' she said to Jill and Graham, 'and it's up to you to look after the others.'

'There're creeks up there', said Aunty Iris, 'where the gold diggers worked. You can get your water out of them.'

'And keep your hats on,' Mum said. 'Especially Derek.'

We wanted to go.

'And if you get lost —'

'We know,' said Jill. 'Find a creek and follow it down to the coast.'

'There's no need to be smart,' said Mum. 'But creeks have to come out somewhere. They'll always bring you back.'

'Be sure you're on your way back by mid-afternoon,' said Aunty Iris. She pointed at the sun. We knew what she meant. None of us had watches.

The track we found was overgrown. It climbed the shoulder of a hill and dropped into a creek, which we followed upstream. There'd been a good track once because it was benched into the bank in places.

'Where does the water go?' asked Derek.

'Maybe it runs into the Mangrove River,' said Graham, 'or maybe it's the beginning of our creek.'

'We'd better draw it on the map,' said Jill. Ann sat, we spread ourselves around her, and she marked in some lines and wrote a few words on the back of the old calendar she'd brought. We all looked at it and agreed it looked right so far, and went on.

The track climbed left out of the creek, went through some big bush, and dived into scrub again. It went on for hours. Where it came out on a clear spur, we could see the sand-hills and the dark line of the cliffs and pōhutukawas, where the bach and the creek must be. We could see the mouth of the Mangrove River and a green patch on the other side: the Wheelers' farm.

Out to sea, the islands were afloat. There was nothing else, not a fishing boat, not a smear of smoke on the horizon.

'Just think,' said Jill, 'the whole Jap fleet could be out there, with a few submarines in here waiting. They could come in at night and land soldiers on Whalers Beach and sail out of sight again, and nobody'd know.'

'What would the soldiers do?' asked Derek.

'Build a camp in the sand-hills and get ready to attack the Bay.'

'But we'd know,' said Derek.

'They'd kill us, and nobody'd know.'

'What about the Wheelers?'

'They're conchies, remember! They'd probably help the Japanese. They might be signalling to their submarines with lights at night.

'Did you know they changed their name before the war?'

'Why?'

'Because their real name was German.'

'What was it?'

'Nitz, or something like that. I forget now, but it sounded German to me.'

'How'd you know?'

'I heard Aunty Iris talking about it to Mum, but they wouldn't tell me anything when I asked.

'They'd guide the Japanese in with torches. It'd be easy for them to land, cover their tracks, and hide in the lupins. They could make a fort and camouflage it. There could be Jap forts all the way around the coast, just waiting for a signal from Tokyo to start fighting.'

We listened to her. She'd worked it all out.

'They could attack the Bay from several directions at once. You just think about it. They'd cut the phone line to Thames, stop any cars, and nobody'd be any the wiser. Those tank traps, they'd use them to stop our Army from coming to save us. By the time the Government found out, it'd be too late.'

'What about our planes?' asked Jimmy.

'What about our planes! How many have we got? Remember the money we sent to buy Spitfires? Well, they're in Britain, not here.'

'That's the New Zealand Squadron,' said Graham.

'Is that Cobber Kain?' asked Jimmy.

'Cobber Kain's dead ages ago.'

'Well, why wouldn't they send them out, if we needed them?'

'Why would they?' asked Jill. 'They wouldn't know about us in Britain anyway.'

Jill seemed to know what she was talking about. We were sitting on the clear spur, the sun was burning down on our hats, the dry grass, and the sea. Cicadas shrilled away in the scrub. When I thought of them, they sounded deafening.

'Wouldn't the Mounted Rifles find out if the Japs were here?' asked Derek.

'They've got their look-out on Maungawhero,' I said. 'They can see the convoys heading out of Auckland, Tim said, so they'd see the Japs too, if they were coming.'

'What if the Japs came at night?' said Jill. I couldn't think of an answer to that.

'In any case,' she went on, 'they're too busy riding their horses up and down the beaches.'

We followed Jill down into another creek, where she lit a fire and hung the billy on a stick over the flames. 'Don't drink cold water,' she said. 'It gives you cramp when you've been tramping.' She'd learned that at Guides.

'Look! Look!' Graham had climbed a heap of broken rock. We climbed it too. He'd found a pair of rails like a little railway line that disappeared into a tunnel.

'An old gold mine!' said Jill.

Inside the tunnel Graham had found a trolley loaded with rocks. 'That's how they got it out of the tunnel,' he said. 'This whole heap must have come out of there.'

'We could hide in there,' said Derek. 'The Japs wouldn't know.'

'It's wet,' said Jill. 'It's dark, and it stinks. They'd have us caught in there. It's a trap, a tunnel! We've got to find something better.'

Graham was trying to get the trolley moving. We all pushed, and its wheels skidded on the rails. Everything was rusty. We rocked it and pushed it backwards and forwards. 'Don't stop!' Graham grunted. 'It's coming!'

The wheels began to turn. We pushed harder, and they turned more easily.

'Stop!' Graham shouted, but the trolley wouldn't. It ran down the rails, which were on a slope, careered over the end of the heap, hung for a moment, as if afloat on the air, and crashed down the face of the tip.

We all yelled and cheered, but Graham said, 'If you'd stopped when I told you, it wouldn't be smashed.'

'Never mind! That's how we'll smash the Japs, if they come bothering us!' Jill said, and Jimmy and Derek cheered. 'Come on,' she said, 'we'll have our lunch and find a better place.'

The track petered out. Perhaps it only came as far as the mine. We couldn't push through the scrub on the other side, and the creek disappeared in little waterfalls.

While Jill and Graham searched a bit longer, we went back to the clear spur, and Ann filled in more details. She drew in the Mangrove River, and Jill came along and made her put in a creek she reckoned she'd seen, one further up.

Back at the bach, we filled in everything we could think of, but when I said we still hadn't found a place to hide from the Japanese, Jill smiled to herself.

'Oh, yes, I have,' she said.

'Where?'

'I've a place picked out,' she said and wouldn't say any more.

CHAPTER TWELVE
Look-outs and Heroes

THE DAY WE WENT TO Whauwhau Beach was so fine that we all sailed around in the dinghy. There was just enough breeze to keep us going, and we sneaked past Lost Bay, under the biggest cliffs where seagulls hung off the tops, not moving their wings, and Ann and I felt dizzy staring up at them.

Graham and Aunty Iris put up the fly. When Jill asked if we could sail across to Maungawhero, Aunty Iris said, 'The wind's not going to come up any more than this, so you might have to row back. Get us a feed of mussels while you're there.'

We landed on the beach under the high peak and collected a good load of mussels. Jill and Graham really wanted to explore the big cave around the cliffs, and they took down the mast, so they could go further in than we'd ever been. Jill said there just might be somewhere inside where we could hide. Jimmy and Derek said they wanted to explore the cave too.

Ann and I were going to have a look up the side of Maungawhero. Graham said there was a lagoon somewhere up there, and there might be caves at the bottom of the rock faces under the peak. He didn't think there was any way to the top from this side.

The first part was easy, up through karaka trees. Now and again we'd look down through their glossy leaves at the beach, and it was always smaller.

'There's nowhere any good up here,' Ann said. 'Graham wants a flat place with firewood and water. He said a cave would help, even a leaning rock wall.'

'We could eat karaka berries,' I said.

'They're poisonous!'

'They used to know how to get the poison out of them. Uncle Dugald told us,' I said.

'Still, don't even touch them,' Ann said. 'They are beautiful though, aren't they! So glossy, you want to pick them.'

Rocks had tumbled between the trees, or the trees had grown between the rocks, we weren't sure. It was harder climbing. We left the karakas and climbed through a belt of scrub, coming out at the base of the bluffs. Heat came off the grey stone. Even from there, the view was huge.

'You can see why they've got a look-out on top,' said Ann.

I went to the left, but found no way up the smooth faces, went back, and found Ann going up a sort of open-sided chimney which ran up as if cut neatly out of the rock. There weren't any footholds, but she'd pushed herself up, her feet against one side, her back against the other.

'Don't fall on me,' I said and followed. There were a couple of places where we rested, but it took less time than we expected. Ann helped me up the last bit, and we stared down the chimney.

'I don't want to go back down that way,' she said.

'I wouldn't have come up it but for you,' I said. 'We'll get down it all right.'

Seagulls circled below. They were tiny dots. The sea was flat, the beach a white curve between green bush and blue water. Sunken reefs showed clearly.

'If there were any submarines, you'd see them easily, the water's so clear,' Ann said. Over the curve of the world, there were the masts and funnels of a big ship.

There was a noise. We spun around. Right behind us was the Mounted Rifles look-out: a rough shelter rather than a hut, a few sheets of corrugated iron for the roof, and walls made out of nīkau leaves, all built on a frame of poles. There were a few bunks and a table inside, nothing else. I noticed the nīkau leaves were fastened so the rain would run down them, and thought I must tell Graham. He'd like that idea.

Behind, there was a horse paddock with slip-rails, and, standing in it, two horses. One whinnied, the noise we'd heard before. Suddenly we were quiet. We tiptoed around the corner of the look-out and saw two men asleep in the sun. Tim was one, the other was one of the men who'd ridden down the creek with him. They each had an empty beer bottle beside them. Stacks of bottles stood against the end of the hut.

We crept away and lowered ourselves down the chimney. I went first and guided Ann's feet. It was quite easy. We didn't talk till we got to the bottom, then Ann laughed and said, 'They couldn't see much, even if they were up there.'

'How would they signal if they did see anything?' I asked. 'I thought they might have a radio.'

'A flag,' said Ann. 'Or smoke.'

'What did I say,' Jill said, when we met them on the beach. 'They've got no show of spotting the Japs coming.'

She said they'd rowed a long way into the cave, but gave up when it went around a few corners and got lower. 'There was no light,' said Graham, 'and nowhere we could hide.'

'It was creepy,' said Jimmy. 'I thought something might pull me out of the boat and under the water.'

Aunty Iris was pleased with the mussels. She said they were always fat from over there. We added their shells to the heap from the years before, and slept under the fly.

Next morning, Mum and Aunty Iris sailed back, and we said we'd hunt for gold mines on the way back. That's when we saw the Mounted Rifles again.

We were on the hills between Whauwhau Beach and the bach, sitting on a huge kauri stump big enough for all of us to walk around. Graham said Uncle Dugald reckoned there was a kauri so big, they'd pitched a tent on its stump and held a dance.

'And now they're all gone,' said Ann. 'They must have been beautiful. The whole Bay must have looked different.'

There was a high, silvery sound that floated where the great trees had once been. Below, where a clearing ran down a gully, a black spot burst out of the bush, bulleted across, and disappeared into the scrub. A group of horsemen, the bugle crying high above their yells, crashed after it.

'Pig hunting and boozing,' said Jill. 'That's how they're going to beat the Japs!'

We made our way down the track to the bach. We were all quiet. Jill was right. The Japs were coming, and we needn't expect much help from the adults. We had to find somewhere to hide.

'Don't forget', Ann said, as we followed the others down the steep steps on to the flat, 'Jill wants to be boss. That's why she wants us to hide away on our own. She'll be able to order us around as much as she likes.' I nodded and looked at Jill's head disappearing below.

'Still,' I said, 'she makes sense.'

There were visitors at the bach, some familiar, some only half-known faces we saw each year at the Bay, but had to be reminded whose they were. We all knew one of them because we were expecting him, our older cousin Rod, who'd begun the fort. He'd been shot down in his plane, and had been expected home for Christmas.

Rod had managed a crash-landing, but his face and hands were burnt when he was helping his crew out of the wreck, Aunty Iris told us. He was given a medal and was coming home a hero. Now, he'd come out in Luke Kelly's boat with a crowd from the Bay. Most of the men were in uniform.

They'd brought a gramophone, and it was playing a song everybody sang that summer. I remember thinking how strange the music sounded, as we went in, while Mum and Aunty Iris were saying, '. . . and this is Jill, and this is Ann . . . say hallo to Mrs Carter; you know Daisy . . .' and we were saying hallo, and kissing faces pushed into ours, shaking hands, and not staring at Rod because they'd warned us his burns were ugly.

He didn't look different, not till he turned and said hallo, and we saw the other side of his face was yellow and puckered, and the eye looked strange. He shook hands with us, or, rather, he touched the hands we put out, as we'd been warned to do. His hands were maimed paws. They looked worse than his face.

'Lucky brats!' he laughed, and his voice was just the same, 'having summer at the bach. I thought about it all the time, the summers we had here.'

'Why don't you stay?' Jill asked, but he had to go back up to Auckland, then people swirled around him, and Mum was giving us something to eat because we were hungry.

We sat on the steps to keep out of the way. Somebody wound up the gramophone and put on the same record. Some sang with it, some pushed back the table and danced on the verandah. There were bottles of beer along the verandah rail.

Rod was dancing with Edna Henderson from the Bay. He couldn't really hold on to her; he just held his hands at her waist, and she had her arms around him. Then Mum sent us to get water. When we came back, we paddled the dinghy across the creek. We were going to the jumping pit, we said. Jill and Graham stayed with the grown-ups.

We looked back. Luke Kelly's dinghy was tied by the steps. The music and voices came across the water. It was strangely noisy.

'Did you see his face!' said Jimmy.

'And his hands!' said Derek.

'He got a medal,' I said.

'Yeah, but he got it for being shot down. He didn't get it for killing any Germans.'

'He got it for saving the other men in his plane,' I said. 'He saved their lives.'

'His face is just the same on one side,' said Ann. 'I knew him at once.'

'He must've killed a lot with his bombs,' said Derek. 'He's been over there for years.'

'They shot him down though. I wonder if he thinks we're losing the war? Come on!' Jimmy shouted and ran to the jumping pit.

'What if we are losing the war?' Ann asked me. 'What if the grown-ups aren't telling us the truth?'

We'd been climbing the hills all morning. After a few jumps, we lay on the floor inside the fort and talked about Rod. I felt tired and fell asleep. So must the others.

Voices were calling when I woke. The dinghy was going out to Luke Kelly's boat. His was already out there. Graham and Jill ran along the beach shouting. Derek and Jimmy leapt down to meet them.

'Don't yell,' Ann said. 'Look!' I joined her, peeping through the only gap in the parapet that faced inland. On a patch of sand two people lay together, Rod and Edna. Their clothes were bright among the lupins.

Ann touched my arm. 'Edna's married,' she said. 'Her husband's overseas.'

I wasn't sure what she meant, just knew something wasn't right. I felt confused and wanted to go, but Ann pulled me back.

'No,' she said. 'Watch!' and we peeped, spying, fascinated, until Rod and Edna went to get up. 'Come on,' Ann said, and we backed away, tiptoeing across the sandy floor of the fort, as if we might be caught and punished. Then we were both scrambling down the other side above the wreck of the scow, leaping, sliding, yelling.

'You had the dinghy,' said Jill, 'and they have to get going.'

As we went towards the mouth of the creek, Rod and Edna came down out of the sand-hills and stood looking at the scow. We waited, and they caught up to us.

I saw Mum look at them, but nobody else seemed to notice anything, then they were gone on the last trip out to the boat. We could hear somebody playing the gramophone with the same record out there.

Luke Kelly started his engine, and we couldn't hear the music any longer. Somebody was helping Rod over the side, then the dinghy was coming back, and the launch disappeared towards the Bay.

We all piled in and rowed up to the bach. It was quiet again, but untidy. Beer bottles stood on the table and rail. We stacked them under the bach, and dried the dishes.

'What a mob!' said Aunty Iris.

'It was lovely to see Rod,' said Mum.

That night, I lay in my bunk and listened to their voices, as they sat beside the fire in the barrel chairs.

'How did you think he looked?' Mum said.

'A lot of his face will clear up in time,' said Aunty Iris. 'Not all of it though. It's his hands that'll be the trouble. The skin looks as if it could just crack open again at any moment. Goodness knows what he'll do for a living. He'll never work on the farm again.'

'Did you hear what he said about our black-out?'

'That it's stricter than Britain's?'

'Yes, and how there's been accidents because of it.'

'Mmm!'

I waited for them to say something about Edna Henderson, but heard nothing more. I wondered what she and Rod had been doing in the sand-hills, why they'd wandered away from the others. They must have gone right down to the mouth of the creek, before they could cross without getting wet through. Nobody could have seen them from the bach.

I was drifting off the sleep again. A little wave made a distant thunder that came closer, like the noise of a train rushing along Whalers Beach from Mangrove River towards the mouth of the creek.

CHAPTER THIRTEEN
Looking After Ourselves

JIMMY WAS SITTING IN THE bottom of the jumping pit, and Jill stood over him and over the rest of us too. 'You saw Rod's face,' she said. 'It could happen to you.'

'He came down in a plane,' said Jimmy. 'Dad got wounded, but he's all right now, Mum said.'

'He's not well enough to write yet, is he!' said Jill. 'Lots of people get wounded and burnt. Not just pilots. That's what war's like. What do you think happens to women and children?'

'Children?'

'Yes, children! They get killed and burned too. That's why you have air raid practices at school. The school committee didn't dig those slit trenches in the horse paddock for nothing.'

'Yes, but — '

'Remember the Germans sank that ship with nearly a hundred children on board. The *City of Benares*. They all drowned. Do you think the Japs'll be any different?'

Jimmy looked angry, the way he did when he was worried. 'Why would they want to kill us?' he yelled.

'Because', said Jill, 'they like killing children. They torture children.'

'How do you know?'

'Because they told us at Guides. And I heard Mum and Aunty Iris talking.'

'It's true,' Graham said. 'The *Herald* says they've done some awful things, atrocities.'

'They chop the heads off their prisoners of war,' said Jill. 'They raped those nurses, then bayoneted them.'

I looked at Ann. She looked away.

'They wouldn't have wanted to live,' said Jill. 'I know I wouldn't.

'So we're going to have to look after ourselves. The

grown-ups aren't much use. The Mounted Rifles are too busy pig hunting. You heard what Tim called them: the Hill-Billies.

'Our soldiers are all overseas, and the Home Guard's not much use.'

'We could hide up in the bush,' said Derek. 'In the old mine.'

Jill said nothing. She knew she'd won. Jimmy was the only one who'd said he wouldn't go, and he was crying now. The bit about Rod's burns had worked. Ann distrusted Jill, but she was scared of the Japs too.

'We'd have to be well hidden,' said Jill. 'We'd need shelter, clothes, food.'

'Lost Bay?' said Derek.

'It's the first place they'd look.'

'We've got the dinghy,' said Graham. 'We could get somewhere in that.'

'Out on the islands,' said Derek.

'Too small,' said Jill. 'They're a trap, like the tunnel. And there's no water. In any case, the grown-ups are going to search the coast for us. We've got to hide from them as well as from the Japs.

'There is somewhere,' she said.

'The cave!' said Derek.

'I'm not saying yet,' said Jill. 'It's got to be a secret, till I've got a plan worked out. And don't you breathe a word to Mum and Aunty Iris!' she said, bending and pushing her face into Jimmy's. He was the one most likely to tell. 'Just remember Rod's face! How would you like to look like that — all over?'

Jimmy stared at her. He shook his head slowly, his eyes brimming. He wouldn't dare say a word.

I knew Jill had been making plans and lists of things we'd need. Luke Kelly had brought out our new stores, and the big food tins and bins were full. Our problem would be how to get away.

That night, Derek jumped while eating dinner. Mum asked if he had toothache, but he said he'd been to the dental nurse just before leaving. He woke crying later, and Mum gave him something, but he kept the rest of us awake. Next morning, he was all right, but he cried again in the night.

'We'll have to take you into the Bay, and over to the Thames,' said Aunty Iris. 'It's not your fault. You couldn't help it.'

So it was decided Mum and Aunty Iris would walk into the Bay with Derek. Mum would pick up the mail, she was still looking for a letter from Dad, and come back. Derek and Aunty Iris would stay the night in the Bay and go over to the dentist. They mightn't be back for several days.

Mum said we'd be all right with Jill and Graham to look after us, but, at the last moment, she started to worry, so we all walked with them as far as the creek at the beginning of Whauwhau Beach.

The three of them set off along the beach. They would climb around the back of Maungawhero, walk along Dumper Beach, then over the hill and down past the cemetery to the jetty and old Henry's ferry.

Usually we took a billy and had a picnic on Whauwhau Beach, then, if old Henry was drunk, we'd boil the billy again and wait for somebody to come over and take us across.

'No swimming without Jill or Graham there,' Mum said, 'and keep in the creek. You hear that, Jill! And keep your hats on.'

They crossed the creek and walked away from us. I thought Jimmy was going to run after them, but they turned and waved, and he waved back. They became dots which danced, disappeared, and appeared again, as the sand grew hot and heat waves began.

Jimmy said he could still see them near the rocks at the far end. When he said they'd gone, we all felt lonely.

'Come on,' said Graham, and we plodded between the walls of tea-tree that crackled with the heat. A big cicada flew with a drumming noise into Ann's hair. I picked it out, and it whirred away noisily. When we reached the shade of the pōhutukawas, going down to the bach, it was like slipping into water.

'Let's go in off the beach,' said Jimmy.

'You heard Mum,' said Jill.

'It's more fun in the waves.'

'I promised Mum we'd keep in the creek.'

'Aw!' But he knew it was no good arguing when Jill had promised.

We swam in the creek. Then Jill and Graham wanted to check what we could take from the bach, so we went to the fort. It was too hot for jumping. Later Jill let us lie inside the mouth of the creek, where cool water came in with the waves, but she wouldn't let us go any further.

'I promised,' she said.

'We can't go without Derek,' Ann said to Jimmy, when he wondered if Jill was planning to run away. In any case, Mum and Derek came back exhausted, late that evening.

There'd been a doctor in the Bay, and he'd taken out Derek's tooth. It was a very small one.

'Thank goodness, for that,' said Mum. 'He saved us going all the way over the hill!'

'Was there a letter from Dad?' I asked.

'No. But there's no service car till tomorrow. It's not running every day now, so Aunty Iris stayed in the Bay, and she'll collect the mail and come back tomorrow night. She won't get here till well after dark, so I'm going to meet her at Whauwhau Beach, and we'll come back together. You'll be all right with Jill and Graham.'

'How will you see?' asked Jimmy.

'I'll take the hurricane lantern,' said Mum. 'Do you know, there's not a single torch battery to be had in the Bay for love nor money! They've all been snapped up by hoarders.'

'Somebody might see you and think you're signalling to the Japs,' said Graham.

'Who is there to see us?'

'Shall we go with you?' Jimmy asked. I could almost hear Jill hold her breath, but Mum said, 'No, thanks. We'll be all right. I'll only be away an hour or two. We'll have an early tea, then you can get yourselves to bed, when it gets dark. I'll make you a cup of cocoa if you're awake when I get back.'

Jill and Graham were looking at the papers she'd brought back.

'The Japs seem to be winning,' said Graham.

'Everyone says they won't get past Singapore,' Mum said.

Next evening, she took the lantern and went to meet Aunty Iris.

Jill was ready with her lists. As she directed us we loaded the dinghy with sacks of food and clothes. We took the big fly. We filled sugar-bags with fishing lines, hooks, sinkers, old knives, billies, mugs, and plates.

She even had a note ready. It said we were going to hide from the Japanese, that we were scared the grown-ups weren't going to look after us, so we were going to look after ourselves and come back when it was all safe. She made us all sign the note, and left it under the tea caddy above the mantelpiece.

The dinghy was heavily loaded. It wouldn't float with all of us in it, so we towed it down to the mouth. I looked back from the bend. The pōhutukawa was losing its last flowers. It looked rusty. The bach was closed and silent. Ann touched me, and I turned and followed her.

Jimmy and Derek were very quiet. We rowed out a few yards and hoisted the mainsail. The gaff pointed up, and the boat started moving. The sea was smooth, with no breakers at all. Jill ordered Ann and me to pull up the jib and steered us into deeper water.

No fishing boats were in sight, and our sails were already disappearing in the darkness above. We were reaching, with a light breeze off the land. Jill wouldn't say where she was heading.

'Gosh!' Jimmy said. 'Mum's going to be mad with you, Jill.'

'She'll get our note.'

'She'll be all alone, just her and Aunty Iris. Perhaps we'd better go back because she'll be lonely,' he said, but Jill steered on into the dark. It was all right for her, she had something to keep her busy. I felt worried about what Mum would say too.

We slid along so smoothly I must have fallen asleep, because I woke, and Ann was spreading sacks over Jimmy and Derek.

'That's better,' Jill said, as Ann came back beside the centrecase with me. Then I heard Graham say, 'We must be off the bar now.'

Jimmy must have woken. 'Is Mum back yet?'

'Not for a while yet,' Jill said.

There was silence. Then Graham was whispering, 'Lucky there's no moon. They might've seen us going past.'

Ann and I sat up and looked into the dark. She grabbed my hand, and I saw it too: a light which, at first, I thought was a star.

'Wheelers'!' said Ann.

We had crossed the bar and were drifting up the Mangrove River.

Book Two
UP THE MANGROVE RIVER

CHAPTER FOURTEEN
Safe from the Japs

W E DIDN'T LOWER THE SAILS in case we made a noise and the Wheelers heard. We sat silent, and the tide carried us upriver.

'They're supposed to have their lights blacked out,' Jill said. 'Conchies!' As if they'd heard her, the light went out.

The river spread before us, a lighter colour than the surrounding hills. With the tide coming in, we weren't likely to run aground. Graham pulled in the mainsheet, and we tacked up towards Mangrove Island. The hermit showed no light. We could smell no smoke. The river was very wide there. We knew other islands lay inside his. We went about and ran under Mangrove Island's dark shape, towards the western side of the river, dropped the sails, and rowed up a channel that wound and bent and opened and closed and opened again. We rowed for hours, it seemed, then, suddenly, there was a beach under pōhutukawas.

'This'll do us tonight,' Jill said.

We lit a fire, while Graham rigged up the fly. Jill had insisted on bringing several bottles of water, and I could see now she was right. We boiled a billyful, had cocoa and the sandwiches we'd brought, and went to bed rolled in our blankets, lying in a row on top of the sacks we'd laid on the sand.

I woke once, and Jimmy was crying. Graham and Jill were talking to him. I could see the mangroves. Stars shone, and the dinghy was lying on mud. Ann mumbled something in her sleep, and Jimmy quietened.

Jill woke us early next morning with the fire going and porridge ready. The milk powder wasn't mixed properly, but we didn't care. Jimmy and Derek were cold, so Jill made them run up and down, loading everything on the boat.

We heaped sand over the fire, and swished branches to hide our tracks. Jill inspected everything and came down to the dinghy brushing out her footprints behind her. She rubbed out the keel mark in the mud and pushed us off, rubbing her feet over our tracks in the mud as we went.

'A couple of tides, and there'll be no sign,' she said.

'Why can't we stay here?' said Derek.

'They'd find us,' said Jill.

'I wouldn't mind Mum finding us,' Jimmy said.

'Not Mum. The Japs!'

Jimmy and Derek disappeared inside big sacks in the bow, as Jill and Graham took an oar each and rowed down the channel to the first branch.

We spent the morning on the rising tide exploring the channels and mangrove islands. We kept out of sight of the main river, but there were miles of bays and inlets on our side, a maze of mangrove channels.

Jill kept standing and looking up at the hills, trying to work out something. The creeks we did find were too obvious. There was nowhere to hide the dinghy where they finished, and we could be caught up them. One finished on a good beach with a little trickle of fresh water. We boiled the billy with wood so dry it hardly smoked, the flames almost invisible in the sun, and had lunch. Then we went on with our search.

'I'm sure I saw a creek head further up,' Jill said. 'I know! I made Ann put it on the map. Where's the map, Ann?'

We found it amongst our gear, under the sacks of food, blankets, and clothes, under the boom, the gaff, and all the other stuff. Jill kept us searching till Ann found it.

'There!' she said. 'It's there somewhere.' I couldn't see that it helped much, just a few pencil marks that went nowhere, but Jill drove us on.

However, we slept on a muddy island that night. We had bread and tinned tongues for tea, and Derek didn't like them. He was sunburnt, and Jimmy grizzled. We were all sick of being in the boat all day. Jimmy had kept wanting to do a piddle and wanted us to land, but Jill made him do it over the side. Then Derek wanted to go ashore. Even Graham seemed to be losing interest in the search for a good camp.

Jill enjoyed it! As we went around another bend, she turned and looked over her shoulder to see if we'd come to a secret island or a hidden creek, but, always, it was just another channel between more mangroves with their dull, green leaves.

There was one place where we couldn't find a channel and had to row along in sight of the river. Ann and I were taking a turn at the oars, when Derek said, 'I can hear something.' We all listened. There was no sound but the drip of our oars.

'It sounded like a boat,' said Derek.

'We'll hide in the mangroves, just in case,' said Jill. 'Turn in!' she ordered.

The mangroves on the edge were little ones, a couple of feet high. Jill jumped out, as we ran in, grabbed the bow, and pulled the dinghy through them. We shot through with a rush, there was a splash, and Jill disappeared. We were floating in a deep channel hidden behind a thick hedge of mangroves. Jill was spluttering beside us. We hooted and let her hold on to an oar. She didn't know whether to be angry, but Graham shouted, 'Quiet!'

From down river came the sound of an engine. We pulled the dinghy around the corner of the channel, so her mast was hidden behind taller mangroves, and ran back down to the hedge.

'It's Wheelers' launch,' Graham said. 'They're looking for us.'

'How would they know?'

'Mum and Aunty Iris could have walked along the beach and swum the river.'

'Let's wave to them!' said Jimmy.

'Are you mad?' Jill shouted. 'They're conchies. You might as well give yourself up to the Japs.'

The launch was coming closer. We threw ourselves down behind a low sandbank. 'Keep your faces down,' said Jill, but Ann and I were behind a log and kept looking out where it forked, through a screen of leaves and branches. I was looking into the eyes of a man standing on the deck, holding the mast. Another sat on the dodger, his legs through the hatch, steering with his feet. I could have hit them with a stone.

The man on deck pointed down and yelled, the boat swung out into deeper water, straightened, and went on up the river. They can't have known the creek was there.

The launch floated on and went out of sight around the shoulder of the next island. We didn't hear the engine any more.

Jill stood up, wet and covered with sand and mud. 'We're going up this creek,' she said. 'It's hidden from the river. We'll find somewhere up there to camp.'

If she hadn't spoken then, I think the rest of us would have rowed out on the river and been found.

'If we can hide from the conchies,' she said, 'we can hide from the Japs!'

'Course we can!' Graham said gruffly, and Jimmy and Derek threw handfuls of mud and chased each other around. We all felt we'd escaped something. We undid the stays and took down the mast and stowed it inside the boat. There was even less room now.

'We're going to find a place to hide from the Japs!' Derek said, and Jimmy repeated it excitedly.

Without bothering to change into dry clothes, her hair hanging in rats' tails, Jill got in and rowed with Graham. The creek wound, just like all the others, through gnarly old mangroves. It was wide enough to take the dinghy easily. Through the clear water, its steep sides disappeared into darkness. The shallows were marked by mangrove roots that stuck into the air like miniature forests of asparagus.

Now and again, we saw a flatty slip off into the green depths of the channel, leaving a smudge of mud suspended in the water. There were oysters growing on some of the mangroves.

'Great country for crocodiles!' Graham said.

On the rising tide, we went deeper into the mangroves. They met above, and we moved on. We came to pōhutukawas, and Jimmy and Derek wanted to get out there, but Jill looked around, shook her head, and rowed on. She said nothing.

It got too narrow to row, so we poled the dinghy and pulled it along on the overhanging branches. 'Just as well we took down the mast,' Jill said, and her voice sounded strange. It was as if we had been travelling for ever along a dark tree-covered tunnel.

'It's getting narrower,' said Jimmy. 'Let's go back.'

'Shut up!' Jill said.

'Shut up yourself,' said Jimmy. 'You're always bossing us around.'

There was a thump. Jimmy blubbered, 'I'm going to go home and tell Mum.'

'How?' Jill said. 'Swim?'

She was standing on the bow, Graham in the stern, shoving with the oars. Ann and I were pulling on branches. It was darker.

Light blazed on us. We came around a bend out of the long tunnel, out of the narrow channel, and into a wide stretch where trees hung down to the water on one side, and grass came down a bank on the other. The grass seemed to go right back to some big tea-tree with the sun on it. It was all light. We blinked our eyes in it.

'How about this!' said Jill.

She shoved the dinghy alongside the bank and we went rushing and yelling across the clearing. The sun shone, the sky was blue, the grass green. On three sides, hills walled and protected us.

As we raced across the clearing, there was a snort, and a black pig shot into the trees. We shouted, and a dozen little ones leapt after her, spraying out of the grass at our feet. We galloped after, but they vanished.

We ran to the top of the clearing. The creek took a

bend through some rocks and finished in a waterfall. From its stone lip, the water fell into a long pool.

'A swimming pool!' said Jimmy.

We looked down the clearing. Jill stood alone, still by the boat, looking towards us. She looked lonely.

Jimmy and Derek ran shouting towards her, telling her about everything at the tops of their voices.

The cliff that made the waterfall walled the top of the clearing. It leaned out and was dry underneath.

'Somebody's camped here,' said Ann.

An old fireplace stood against the cliff, so old there were no ashes, just a stain of darker rock where the smoke had once risen. I stared at the sign of older people, till Ann touched me. 'Come on,' she said softly, and we went to help unload.

'I'm hungry,' Jimmy was saying.

'Me too,' said Derek.

'We're all hungry,' said Jill, 'but we'll just have to wait till we get unloaded.'

'What've we got to eat?' said Jimmy.

'You and Derek get some dry tea-tree for the fire,' said Jill. 'Ann, how about you and George making some fried scones!'

It was her best idea yet! Ann lit our first fire under the cliff, and we fried the scones in our big frying pan. As they cooked, Jill and Graham staggered up with gear.

'I saw oysters down on the mangroves,' Jill said.

'And pipis in the river,' said Graham.

'There'll be flounders among the mangroves.'

'And we can catch fish in the river.'

'We need a net,' said Jill.

'We can make one with flax,' said Ann, busy with the scones. 'There's plenty up here.'

'I wonder if Mum's looking for us?' said Jimmy, staring at the scones cooking.

'She'll have all the fishing boats in the Bay out searching,' Ann told him.

He smiled. 'But what if the Japs have come?'

'Then they'll be prisoners now. But they won't tell the Japs about us.'

'Wouldn't we hear them shooting?'

'Not up here we wouldn't. Here!' Ann put a couple of fried scones on a plate for Jimmy and Derek. Jill had even remembered the golden syrup.

Fried scones never tasted so good! We ate them, dripping with golden syrup, until we were full and lay in the sun on the clearing. Jill had found us the perfect campsite. We were safe from the Japs!

CHAPTER FIFTEEN
Giant Sprats and Pipis Galore

GRAHAM CHOPPED SOME LONG TEA-TREE poles, and we helped drag them down. Jill wanted a camp out on the clearing, but he said the place to build was under the cliff.

'There's one wall and half a roof already, with the cliff,' he said. Graham could see things like that. Jill didn't like the idea, but I don't think she understood what he meant.

'The water will come down the side of the cliff when it rains,' she said.

'No, it's dry,' said Graham. 'See, there's nothing growing on it, so the rain can't come down it. If it did, there'd be fern and moss all over it.

'See, there's been other camps here too.'

Jill didn't like it, but she pretended to agree.

We helped Graham lean the poles against the cliff and dig their ends in the ground. He made them firm with a stake either side, so they couldn't move. When we spread the big fly over the frame, he put Jimmy up on his shoulders and tied it as high as it would go. It stretched tight, a sloping wall against the leaning wall of the cliff. Even Jill had to admit it made a good shelter. Rain couldn't get in, and there was enough room for all of us to stretch out in our blankets, with space for the stores.

We went to sleep early, leaving Graham and Jill talking by the fire against the cliff.

'We can hide the dinghy', I heard Jill say, 'under the trees. The tent'll be harder. It'll show up.'

'Show up?' said Graham.

'Yes, from a plane. The Japs have got planes. They'd find us easily enough, if they saw the boat and the tent.'

I thought of the newsreel of planes machine-gunning refugees and knew we must hide the camp first thing tomorrow.

Jill had us up working before daylight. 'We've got to hide the tent', she said, 'from Jap planes.' We'd all seen the newsreel, so nobody argued.

'We could do with another axe,' Graham said, as we cut longer poles. He propped them over the fly, tying leafy branches along till it disappeared. It still looked pretty obvious to me, but Jill said it would look like just another patch of scrub from a plane. Ann and I moved the dinghy under the trees.

'What if somebody comes up the creek?' Ann asked.

'It's hidden from the river,' said Jill, 'but if somebody found it and came up, there's nothing we could do.'

'We'll put a boom across,' said Graham, 'down in the darkest part of the tunnel under the trees. It'll stop anybody coming up, even if they find the creek. I can make it look like a tree fallen right across.'

'But we'd still have to get past.'

'It'd swing from one end', said Graham, 'with a rope.' He thought for a moment. 'I can rig it up easily.'

I could see Jill didn't understand him, but she nodded as if she did. 'Come on, everybody,' she yelled. 'Breakfast!'

We ran for the camp. Derek and Jimmy had made porridge.

'Good cooks!' Jill said.

'Dad made us learn,' said Derek. 'He had to learn after Mum died.'

'I wonder if he knows we've run away,' said Ann. 'He'll blame Graham.'

'He'll get the blame because he's the eldest,' said Derek.

Graham said nothing, and his face looked just the same, but we all knew Uncle Paul was hard on him. Mum said it wasn't easy for a man, bringing up children, so she said we had to understand Uncle Paul when he lost his temper.

'He'll be too busy with the Japs to worry about us,' said Jill.

'I wonder if they've come yet,' said Jimmy.

'We'd have heard their guns,' Derek said, and he and

Jimmy dive-bombed and machine-gunned each other. 'Kapow! Kapow! Ah-ha-ha-ha-ha!'

Jill watched them a while. 'If you hear a plane,' she said, 'put the fire out. We'll bring some sand up from the river and keep it by the fire. Just dump it on and smother it.'

'Why not water?' asked Jimmy.

'Sand's better. We used it at Guides to put out incendiary bombs. Somebody tried to put one out with water, and it made a mess and just went on burning. Sand stops smoke too.'

'Do you have E.P.S. wardens?' Ann asked her.

'Yes, they come around and check to see if your lights are showing.'

'Uncle Dugald says every Peeping Tom in the country's become an E.P.S. warden,' I said.

Derek asked, 'What's a Peeping Tom?'

'A dirty old man who looks in your window while you're undressing!' said Ann, and Jimmy and Derek shrieked and jumped around undressing and looking in windows. The rest of us laughed, but Jill was annoyed.

'Uncle Dugald's got no right, saying things like that.'

'He told Mum the Home Guard and the E.P.S. are more dangerous than the Japs,' I said.

'Nonsense!' said Jill. 'Anyway, if anybody hears a plane, tip the sand over the fire and keep out of sight under the tent or a tree. If you're in the open, keep still. Whatever you do, don't look up. They can see you from high up in the air, and they'll come down and machine-gun you. They told us that at high school in our air raid practices.'

We'd finished our porridge and were drinking mugs of tea. Jill let us have one piece of toast each. We had to ration the bread to make the flour last longer, she said. The sun was on the clearing now.

'We'll go down the creek,' Jill said. 'We've got to start looking for food, that's our next job. Somebody can look for pipis, somebody else can get oysters off the mangroves. Graham and I'll look for flatties.'

Together, Ann and I said, 'Bags we look for pipis.' We

wanted to explore the banks along the edge of the mangroves, and we knew Jill and Graham would get the spears.

There was lots of room in the dinghy now. It took less time to go down the creek, even though we got stuck twice and had to work the dinghy backwards and forwards around a couple of tight bends. I was getting out to push off the mud, when Jill screamed at me, 'Stay where you are! You'll get covered in mud!' Ann grinned, without looking at me.

Further down, the sides of the channel were mud walls standing high above us.

'What if a plane came now?' Jimmy asked.

'Sit still and don't look up,' said Jill.

We twisted along the creek. There was a flash of white shells and sand instead of mud, and Jill ran the dinghy into the side.

'Derek, you and Jimmy can get out here and start collecting oysters. Look! There's some over there on that mangrove. Find a rock each, and you can knock them off and put them in your sugar-bags.'

Ann and I took a kerosene tin and a couple of sugar-bags, before she could start giving us orders.

'Keep an eye on the tide,' Jill yelled, as we pushed through the mangroves. 'It's turning, so you haven't got long. Keep a watch out for boats. They'd see you before you saw them. What are you doing with that jag, George?'

'There might be some sprats.'

'You won't need that. Put it back in the boat.'

But I kept going, as if I hadn't heard her, and joined Ann, who was poking her head through the low hedge of mangroves and looking up and down the river. Our creek didn't have a mouth at all; it just spread out through the mangroves. That's why it was so well hidden.

'What are you grinning about?' Ann asked.

'I was just thinking about the way Jill pulled the dinghy through the mangroves and fell into the creek.'

'Look! What's that?'

'What?'

'That white thing!'

'Just a big log shining in the sun,' I said.

'It looked like a boat. Come on!'

We stepped out of the mangroves and ran across the bank, feeling exposed. Ann dipped the kerosene tin full of water and swished it against the bank. There were more pipis than sand: they came rolling out, fat, round, and thick.

'Why do we call them pipis?' Ann said. 'Up in Auckland, some people call them cockles.'

'I don't know. I'll hold this open, and you shovel them in with the tin.' We half-filled our sugar-bags and the kerosene tin and hid them behind the mangroves. We could see Jill and Graham further down. The tide had turned and was coming in. We had time to have a good look around.

Sandbanks showed everywhere. We were on the edge of the pipi bank that the launch had almost hit. The wide, shining, lake-like river had shrunk. It was a different place. In a few hours it would be different again.

An empty shell lifted on the edge of the returning water, floated, and drifted. I went to throw a stick at it, but Ann said, 'See how far it floats.' It drifted into deeper water, turned on a little current, and went further out, but it still floated.

'I wonder how long we'll live here,' Ann said.

'Till the Japs have gone.'

'How will we know that?'

'Oh, we'll know.'

'How?'

'We could put up the mast and sail down the river. Check the Wheelers and see if there's Japs there.'

'Mrs Wheeler wouldn't be friendly with the Japs,' said Ann. 'I liked her.'

'So did I. And Simon. I don't care if the rest of them are conchies.'

We were sitting on the sandbank, watching the tide creep closer to our toes.

'Look!'

'What?'

'Something flashed down there. There! Again!'

I unrolled my jag with its three hooks lashed back to back, and threw it in. I jagged with the long handle. Nothing happened. I jagged again. The line ripped the water. There was a touch and a flash of silver.

'You hit something!'

I pulled in, threw the line out deeper, and jagged again. Something heavy kicked as I pulled it in: a silver sprat bigger than anything we'd seen in the bach creek or jagged off the wharf at the Bay. I took the hook out of its tail, and admired it, while Ann caught another.

'What are they?' she asked.

'I don't know. Giant sprats?'

We caught about twenty. 'Plenty of food here,' Ann said. 'Giant sprats and pipis galore!'

The others were at the dinghy. We carried the pipis back and heard Jill telling off Derek and Jimmy for fooling around.

'You're covered in mud and you've got hardly any oysters.'

'They were too hard to knock off,' said Jimmy.

'You'll have to work if you want to eat here,' said Jill. 'Hit harder, or go hungry . . .'

Maybe she was annoyed because they hadn't got a single flatty. Graham said the tide was out too far. 'In a while,' he said, 'when it's creeping across the mud, that's the time.'

'There's a good feed anyway,' Jill said when she saw the pipis.

'There's lots more,' we said. 'They're thick!'

'We can't live on pipis,' Derek said, 'even if you can, George.'

I was grinning at him, when Ann ran back and returned with our giant sprats dangling from the flax we'd threaded through their gills.

'Heck! Where'd you get them?'

'Little mullet!' said Graham.

'We jagged them,' said Ann. 'And we know where there's more.'

'They're good smoked,' said Graham. 'Aunty Iris's favourite.'

'Can we smoke these?'

'No trouble,' he said. 'I'll make a frame.'

Jill had already snatched my jag. 'We'll get some more,' she said, and Graham disappeared after her through the mangroves.

'They have all the fun, because they're the biggest,' Derek said.

The tide was racing in now. The sandbanks were shrinking, the water was rising in the channels and spreading across the mud to the mangroves. One of their berries, a khaki nut of folded leaves, floated past my foot. Jimmy and Derek started splashing the mud off themselves. They were going to get wet through.

Ann and I took the spears and slid across the mud, the little spears of the mangrove roots sticking up between our toes. Ann froze. I knew she'd seen one. Wham! 'Good shot!' I said. We sneaked across a flat where the water was about six inches deep. Ann got another, then I got a big one.

By the time we heard Jill's angry bellowing, we'd got five. They'd got some more mullet, but she was angry with us for keeping them waiting.

'Don't you dare wander off like that,' she said, but didn't know what to say when she saw our flatties.

Graham just said, 'I thought it might be better when the tide was in a bit. Good on you.'

'Come on,' Jill said. 'We'll go home and have a feed.'

The tide carried us up the creek. Graham saw a place where he could put a boom, as we went through the dark stretch.

'We can live here for ever,' Jill said, as we unloaded pipis, mullet, and flatties, and a couple of sugar-bags of sand for the fire, 'with food like this!'

CHAPTER SIXTEEN
The Garden of Eden

W E PICKED OUT A BILLY of little potatoes from the sack we'd brought and, when they were almost done, steamed some mullet on top. They were so good, we sucked their tiny bones. Even Derek enjoyed them. We lay on the clearing stuffed full and couldn't move. Only Derek crawled into the shade of the cliff.

'What'll we do with the pipis?' I asked Jill.

'Don't talk of food,' she said.

'Should I put them in the creek?'

'Shut up and let me sleep.'

Graham had made a rack of tea-tree rails high above the fire. The rest of the mullet lay on it, split open, smoke lifting about them.

'Once they're dry,' he said, 'we'll hang them under the cliff. They'll keep for ages.'

'Mum said, when they were kids, the people from up the Bay river used to come down and dry fish in long rows like clothes-lines,' Jill told us. 'They camped across the river from Aunty Iris's, up from Back Bay, by the little creek there.'

'Probably mullet.'

'She said you've got to dry them or smoke them cold, if you want to keep them.'

'Mmm.' Graham sounded half-asleep. It was warm, and I felt comfortable. I could feel myself sinking down into sleep.

A fly kept crawling on my nose. I brushed it away, but it landed again. It crawled across the side of my face, and I raised my hand slowly and whacked it hard. I'd got it. I settled back, but a moment later it was back again. This time, I sat up, and saw it was Ann tickling me with a bit of grass. She tiptoed away, and I followed.

Jimmy opened his eyes and watched us go, but didn't stir.

I followed Ann to where the cliff disappeared into the bush. 'I found a track this morning,' she whispered.

If it was a track, it had long grown over, but Ann pointed at something. 'See!'

'What?'

'Oh, use your eyes! That log. It's been sawn through.'

The end was flat, the straight edge of a saw cut, even though the log was old and rotting.

'Somebody might have lived here then.'

'Of course they did! Can't you feel it? They might have had a farm here, in the olden days . . . It's sad, isn't it?'

'I suppose so. How'd they get here?'

'Up the creek. It was probably open then. You know how the bach creek opens and closes.'

I did. It often blocked after a storm, and we'd dig a channel through to let the water go.

The track led us into light, what seemed another clearing, but it was just the trees that were different, smaller and lighter coloured than the bush we'd come through.

'It's an orchard!'

'Apples!' Ann cried, and there was a roar of woofs and snorts, as a mob of pigs struggled to their feet and took off.

'They were asleep!' she laughed, 'full of apples and plums.'

'We could catch them and have wild pork.'

'With apple sauce.'

She was climbing a plum tree. I swung up beside her, and we ate till we fell on the ground, full of plums on top of mullet and potatoes. 'I think I've got the collywobbles,' Ann groaned.

I looked at her. As we'd bitten into the luscious globes of the yellow plums, their skins had split. We lay in the golden-green light coming through the leaves and licked the juice, like syrup, off ourselves.

'Look at the apples!' Ann said.

'I can't crawl to them,' I said. 'I'm drunk on plums!'

Jimmy and the others found us there, and we explored the orchard. There were grapes, still hard, and Graham found some apricot trees.

'They only grow where there's gold in the ground,' he said. 'Aunty Iris said that.'

'Is it an old gold camp?' we asked. 'Do you think the cliff's full of gold?'

'More likely an old farm,' said Graham. 'Maybe one of the returned soldiers walked off after the Great War.'

'Ooh! Pigs' muck!' Derek had walked in some.

'Could we catch one?' I asked Graham.

'Maybe. There must be a way of trapping them. It'd be easy if we had a dog.'

'We'll be your dogs,' said Jimmy.

'Pig dogs get ripped and torn.'

'We'll rip and tear the pigs!'

'There must have been a house,' said Ann. 'I just know it. One like Mrs Cross's.'

'It might have burnt down,' I said.

'I don't want it burnt down,' she said angrily. 'I want to find it.' But there was no sign of a house, though we looked in the bush behind the orchard.

We went back and swam in the pool and stood under the waterfall. The water was different. It wasn't as easy to float in, and your skin didn't crackle when it dried. Beneath the rocks, where the dinghy was tied up, it was brackish.

'That's because the tide comes right up,' Jill said. 'Always drink water from above the rocks,' she said. 'Salt water makes you go mad.'

'We went to the flicks,' Derek said, 'and it was about some people in a lifeboat. They'd been torpedoed, and one of them drank salt water and went mad. He jumped over the side.'

'Did they have anything to eat?' I asked.

'Just each other,' said Derek.

'Lucky we've got plenty to eat,' said Graham, 'or we'd have to eat each other.'

'Who'd we eat first?' asked Jimmy.

'You because you're the youngest, and you'd be good eating because you're quite fat.'

'Derek's only a few weeks older!'

'We'd start eating him a few weeks after we'd finished you,' said Graham. 'Mmm!' He licked his lips.

'Aw!'

We'd dried, lying on the grass, and it was time for tea. The mullet had gone brown, and we wanted to try them, but Jill said they had to be saved.

'We'll have pipis,' she said. 'There's watercress across the other side. It should taste all right with them, and it'll mean we're getting some greens.'

Ann and I picked the cress. It grew in a little creek under the cliff. We had to get wet again to cross the creek and reach it.

'It'll be good if we all like it,' Ann said.

'Jimmy won't like it.'

'The nurse came to school and told us about eating green veges,' Ann said. 'She reckoned brown bread was best.'

'We've only got white flour.'

'Yes, but we've got fresh fruit, and fish, and watercress. And Graham might catch a pig.'

We were eating watercress while picking it. 'If you eat enough', I said, 'it makes your pee turn green.'

'Well ours will be bright green!'

The pipis had spat out their sand, and Jill and Graham had cooked them. Now they tipped them out, a steaming hot heap. We flicked them out with our fingers and raced to see who had the most empty shells in front of them. Jill stopped us gulping them down and made us eat some watercress as well. Jimmy didn't like his, but he ate it because Jill wouldn't give him a slice of bread.

Graham was going to throw the shells in the creek, but Jill said, 'Put them in the boat.'

'Why?'

'They're just tonight's. There's another lot to eat tomorrow. In a couple of weeks, you'd be able to see them from a plane. We've got to think of things like that.'

She let us have half a mullet each. They were a lighter colour inside, oily, and sweet.

'We'll keep smoking the rest till they're cured,' she said. 'There'll be times when we'll need a store of smoked fish, when we can't catch anything in the river, and the fruit'll be finished. We really need a garden.

'The Japs might patrol the river.'

'We could fish at night,' I said.

'You need a light for flatties at night,' said Jill. 'Oh, I forgot the flatties. We were going to try them as well.'

'We can have them for breakfast,' said Graham.

'We'll have to bake bread tomorrow,' said Jill. 'There's only one of Mum's loaves left.

'We've got flour and yeast,' said Ann. 'We'll make some in the billies. I wish we had a camp oven.'

'Well, I couldn't remember everything!' Jill barked.

'That's all right,' Ann said. 'I like baking bread, that's all. George and I'll make it, if you like.'

We had flounder for breakfast. They were all right smoked, but I preferred them fresh. When the others went up to have another look around the orchard, we were already mixing the yeast into the flour. We'd set it to rise earlier, and it looked good. Graham had brought up a plank from the river, and we kneaded and rolled the dough on that.

We worked away, punching and pulling it around, and the satisfying smell rose from the dough. I liked making bread with Ann.

'It's like the Garden of Eden,' she said. 'You know, in the Bible. All the fish and fruit and pipis. There's everything. And it's so pretty. We've got the swimming pool, and the waterfall. We couldn't have found a better place! It's too good to be true!' But she cried as she said it.

CHAPTER SEVENTEEN
The Hermit

I CUDDLED ANN. 'I'M ALL right,' she said, but she hugged me and cried some more.

When she rubbed her eyes, I said, 'You've got a big piece of dough on your eyebrow. No, there, that side.'

'It's just something about this place,' she said. 'Something sad. You know what I mean. As if something's happened here, or it's going to happen.'

'Tell me while I put the bread on,' I said. 'It's risen enough.' While I hung the billies over the fire and heaped coals on their lids, Ann crouched close to me and thought.

'How long do you think we can last here?' she asked.

'Till the Japs have gone, I suppose.'

'We'll be out of potatoes before long.'

'There's a whole sack.'

'We'll have to plant some, and we'll eat the others quickly.'

'Mrs Wheeler wouldn't mind if we stole some from her garden, specially not if the Japs are going to get all their veges anyway.'

'We don't even know if the Japs are coming!'

'Nobody's stopping them,' I said, but I knew what Ann was thinking. She had her doubts about Jill, that's what she was saying.

'I wonder about Dad, all alone up in Auckland,' she said, 'and Aunty Iris, and Aunty May, how they're feeling.'

'If the Japs are here, they'll be pleased we're safe,' I said.

'But they don't know that,' Ann said, and she cried again.

'If we don't see anything of the Japs, we can always go back to the bach.'

'Can we?' said Ann. 'Do you think Jill will let us?'

'She can't stop us. We can slip off any time we like.'

'Promise!'

'Promise!' She hugged me. 'Now, let's have a swim, then it'll be time to put on another batch. It won't take long to cook in billies, not as long as in the big camp oven.'

The others straggled back with a kit of plums and ripe peaches, but they'd found no other sign of the people who'd planted the orchard.

'Gee, that bread smells good!' said Jimmy.

'Leave it alone,' Jill said. 'We won't eat it till it's cooled. It'll last longer.'

'Mum always lets me have some hot.'

'We haven't enough flour for you to be making a meal out of bread,' Jill said, 'so stop your grizzling.'

'We made two batches,' said Ann. 'These are cool, so we can cut one of them.'

'All right,' Jill grunted.

'What about when we run out of flour?' I asked her.

'I've been thinking of that,' she said. 'We'll sneak out to Mangrove Island and see what the hermit's up to. He's got a garden out there, Luke Kelly told Graham, and he must have stores. We might be able to get something from him.'

'What, tell him we're here?'

'No, not that. But we could have a look.'

'What if the Japs have caught him?' asked Jimmy.

'How would they know he's there?'

We had smoked fish, plums, peaches, and a slice of bread for lunch, hung up the food in sacks, where it would be safe, and dropped down the creek in the dinghy.

The tide was in far enough for us to get along inside the mangroves until we were opposite the hermit's island. There, we hung on to branches and searched the river for life. Jimmy had the best eyes, but he saw nothing.

'Make sure,' said Jill. 'We know the Japs are cunning.'

Jill and Graham pulled strongly, using both pairs of oars. The sun was hot. There was no wind. Suddenly we were uncovered in the middle of the huge river. I saw water torn up by machine-gun bullets and the shadow as a plane banked and swept over us.

'It's just a gannet', Ann said, 'feeding in the river.' She

111

nudged me and grinned, but none of us was happy out there on the broad face of the water.

We came under the island, Jill and Graham grunting on each stroke, and dived into a channel. The rest of us pulled on branches, while they ran in their oars and slumped over them. Round a bend, and hidden, we slipped under a tall mangrove and nosed on to mud.

Jill got her breath back. 'We'll go that way,' she whispered. 'You and George go that way.

'Go very slowly. No noise. Don't talk. Just see if you can find his hut, and the garden, that's all.'

'What if he sees us?'

'Tell him Mum and Dad are fishing down the river. Don't tell him your names.

'You two', she whispered, 'turn the dinghy around very quietly, and keep her afloat. Don't leave her. We may have to go in a hurry!'

Ann and I slid across the mud, as she and Graham went the other way around the island. We skidded and ducked under the mangroves, feeling their roots between our toes and under our feet, watching the crabs running sideways before us. Where there was shell and sand, it was firm, but there seemed no dry part to the island, until we saw a jumble of logs and sticks ahead. The mud sucked us back, but we reached firm shells, and there were green reeds like thick grass. Ann helped me, as I climbed a log and peeped at sand and grass on the other side where the mangroves thinned out and small ngaio trees grew.

There were no footprints. The sandbank curved away through the mangroves like a crocodile's tail, and we followed it.

Something moved. Ann giggled and pointed. Two shags perched on a branch wobbled their heads, sinking them on their necks, holding their wings out. I knew they were drying their feathers. Aunty Iris said they didn't have oil on them, so they could dive and chase fish easily. It's why they swim with only their heads sticking out of the water. All that flashed through my head, as I realized they'd scared me and I'd jumped, and that's why Ann had giggled.

The dead branches beneath the shags' perch were splashed white with their droppings. They flew off, dropping from their branch and pounding the air with their wings, looking like sinister bombers.

'Keep still!' Ann whispered. 'The hermit might have noticed them.' The air stunk with their droppings. We stood for ages, and moved on.

Two blackbacks stood on an old kauri head that must have been swept up in a storm. From the top branch, they could see out over the whole of the island. I thought, if I were the hermit, I'd use the kauri head as a look-out myself.

The blackbacks took off. We sneaked on. Whoosh! I felt it brush my hair, as one dived, squawked, banked, and dived again. We got under a mangrove just as the other dived. They hung squawking on the air, staring down at us.

'They're as bad as dogs barking,' Ann muttered. 'The hermit must know there's somebody on the island now.'

I held a broken branch above us, and we stepped out. The blackbacks peeled off like fighter planes, but they dived at the branch instead of our heads and then gave up. We were looking for a place to wait for a few minutes, to let things quieten down, when we stumbled on the hermit's garden.

Cabbages, carrots, lettuce, tomatoes, and beans grew in rich, black soil. A spade stood there, as if the hermit had just stuck it in and gone a minute ago. The air smelled of soil and vegetables.

We followed a hard path, not leaving footprints, and came on the hut suddenly. Even though we were expecting it, even though we were creeping carefully, we stumbled on it suddenly, on the highest part of the island, among mangroves, logs, reeds, and ngaios. I thought it was another kauri head polished white by the sun and wind and rain, then saw the plank walls, the corrugated iron roof rich with rust. Two windows had shutters propped open on sticks, and sacks for curtains. There was a real door, wide open. One end looked as if it were all chimney — also made of corrugated iron, rusty and filled with holes.

We froze. Jill and Graham stood looking caught. They didn't move, just stared down at the ground. They looked odd, as if they daren't move because the hermit had a gun on them, I thought, and I sank, dragging Ann down with me. I'd already begun trying to crawl backwards, when Jill looked up. Her face was white.

She looked straight at us. 'Keep back!' she said, but we'd seen she wasn't a prisoner and stepped forward, and it was too late. She and Graham were standing staring down at the hermit's body. He'd been dead some time.

'What happened to his eyes?' I asked.

'Blackbacks,' said Jill.

'How'd he die?'

'The Japs must've shot him.' Jill turned and ran away on a track into the mangroves. I saw her stumble and bend over, and we could hear her being sick. We stared at the hermit, then Jill was calling, 'Quick! Quick!'

She was at the end of the path, by a deep channel dug by hand.

'Look!' she said. 'Just what we want!'

A long, flat-bottomed punt was tied there. A box of fishing lines sat in it, a knife stuck behind a rib; there was a pair of oars, a sack to sit on, and an anchor. But Jill pointed in the stern at a net.

'We'll get all the fish we want with that!' she said. Suddenly she was all right again and started giving orders.

'Get a spade,' she said. 'There must be one in the hut.'

I got the spade from the garden, Graham found a shovel, and we dug a grave. It was easy digging, just sand and mud. We rolled him in with the spade and shovel. There was an awful noise.

'Just the gas coming out,' said Graham.

He fell in face-down, one arm jammed above his head. Graham pushed it down with the shovel. I was pleased his face was hidden, and the eye sockets.

'Poo, he stinks!' I said.

'Cover him!' Ann and I took turns shovelling the sand

114

back. Jill said, 'Our Father Which Art in Heaven', and, when we'd finished, she made us all sing 'God Save the King'. 'He might have died fighting for New Zealand,' she said.

We shovelled sand where he'd been lying, and the flies started disappearing. We stamped the grave flat and scattered shells and leaves around. Soon, nobody would know a dead man lay there.

'We'd better put a cross,' said Ann.

'Then the Japs would know we've been here,' said Jill. 'They're bound to come back.'

'They'll still know he's gone,' said Ann. 'What difference does it make!' But Graham had already made a cross with a couple of sticks tied together with fishing line. He gave it to Ann, and she knelt and stuck it in the sand.

'Why would they kill him?' she asked. 'Just a lonely old hermit . . .'

We hadn't touched him with our hands, but we went down to the water and scrubbed them with handfuls of sand.

CHAPTER EIGHTEEN
The Japs

INSIDE THE HUT, EVERYTHING WAS tidy: a stack of dry wood by the fireplace, a bunk with sacks for blankets, a table under one of the windows, a big home-made chair covered in sacks, shelves and shelves of stores, and goods of all kinds. Boxes and tins and jars of hooks, and food, and nails, string, vegetable seeds, spears, knives, forks, spoons, mugs, plates, tools, sails, tarpaulins, old clothes: it was just like the bach.

'We've got everything we need here,' said Jill, and she made us load the punt with big tins of flour, sugar, and porridge. There were boxes of tea, cases of beans and spaghetti, enough to keep us eating for years.

'The Wheelers used to bring his stores out for him,' said Graham.

'What'd he do for money?' I wondered.

'Luke Kelly called him a remittance man: he got money sent to him to stay away from home.'

'Where'd he come from?'

'England.'

'It's not right to live by yourself. He must have done something terrible,' said Jill.

'It'd be fun,' said Ann, and her face lit up, as it did when she was reading. 'Living like Robinson Crusoe, with only the seagulls to talk to.'

'Look what they did to him in the end,' said Jill.

I didn't want to think about it.

'We'll row the punt around,' said Jill. 'You two go back to the others, meet us at the top of the island, and we'll row back together. If anything happens, we can leave the punt in the mangroves and get in the dinghy.'

This time I was ready for the blackbacks and threw a stick at them. I hated them. As they took off, I looked at their yellow beaks, at the red fleck near the end. They hung on the wind, watching, but didn't chase us.

We told Jimmy and Derek that the hermit was dead and buried, nothing more.

Back at camp, with both boats tied beside the bank, and the stores in the tent, Jill said, 'We'll get everything from Mangrove Island. We'll strip the hut empty.'

'That'll mean a fair few trips,' Graham said.

Jill nodded. 'If somebody finds he's gone, and half his stuff missing, they'll start looking for him and find us. If we take everything, they're more likely to think he's just moved. That's the sort of thing a hermit might do.'

'What if it's the Japs?' I asked.

'They might only have wounded him. Perhaps they didn't know they'd killed him.'

'But he's lived on Mangrove Island for years,' said Graham.

'It's our best chance,' Jill said.

'What if we're seen?'

'We won't be. We'll go at night, take both boats, and come back on the incoming tide, so it'll help us.

'We'll sleep during the day.' Jill had it all worked out. 'Tide's full about midday, so if we row out after dark, we can load the boats and be home about midnight.

'If the Japs killed the hermit, they'll be patrolling the river during the day. That's why we can't risk crossing in daylight again. If he just died, the Wheelers will come up because they won't have seen him for a week or so. That's why we must get all his stuff now. Everything!

'We'll rest this afternoon, go out tonight, and bring back a load.'

It wasn't hard to see. We sneaked down the other side of the island, listening for Jap patrol boats, and followed the punt up his channel in the dark. I didn't like walking past his grave, but forgot it, as we carried load after load to the boats.

The dinghy grounded for a while, but the rising tide lifted it off. Jill found a couple of bins filled with potatoes and carrots packed in sand. We filled some sacks and had to carry them between us. We put a huge camp oven over the fire, half-filled with potatoes. When they were done, we mashed them, tipped in a couple of tins of corned beef, mixed in chopped-up onions, and ate while the tide rose.

It was a warm hut. Jill sat in his chair, the rest of us on his bunk and around the fireplace.

'We could stay here for ever,' Jimmy said.

Jill snorted. 'They'd find us and shoot us, like the hermit.'

We must have fallen asleep. Ann woke me. 'Shh!' she said, and I followed her down past the hermit's grave. There was no wind. The sky was full of stars. Some seemed just above the mangroves.

'I'm sure I heard something,' Ann whispered. Far away, at the back of my mind, it seemed, there was the slightest sound. I closed my eyes and concentrated.

'Jill! There's a boat! Jill!'

She came awake at once. Derek and Jimmy tried to go back to sleep, but she dragged them up and pushed them stumbling to the boat. 'Grab what you can!' she shouted. Ann took off with a sack of something, and I followed with another, heaving up the camp oven with my other hand. Graham and Jill followed, dragging sacks of gear along the ground to hide our tracks. We rowed around the head of the island, stopped and listened. There were gurgles and splashes in the dark around us. A motor sounded clear.

'Into the mangroves!' Jill hissed. The punt ran in easily. The dinghy was harder to work in because it drew more water, but the tide was high, and we got behind some mangroves just as the sound of the engine chugged past the island and up the river. Graham whispered in the punt beside us, 'Sounds like a big boat.'

After a long wait, we pushed out and rowed straight across and into the mangroves on our side, listening all the time for the returning boat. We rowed along the open spaces behind the mangroves, Jimmy and Derek asleep in their sacks in the stern. Both boats were heavily loaded. Jill and Graham slid over a sandbank that we couldn't clear in the dinghy and caught up to us, just as a long finger of light poked down the far side of the river, swept across and on to the island. It went out for a minute, and sprang on again, right upon us, or on the mangroves outside.

'Shut your eyes and keep still,' said Graham. 'Don't look, even if they come towards us, or they'll see your eyes.'

We kept our heads down, and nobody moved. The light swung away and up the river.

'Shove the dinghy behind that bank!' said Jill. We jumped over the side and hid its white hull, just before the searchlight swept over us again.

'They're going down the other side of the island,' said Graham. 'They can't see us now. Let's go!'

When they played it up our side again, we were well-hidden behind a thick belt of mangroves, heading for our creek. Although wet through, Ann and I rowed so hard, we were warm. Derek and Jimmy slept through the lot.

While Jill and Graham spread tarpaulins over the boats, we got Jimmy and Derek up to the camp and into bed. We had the fire going and put on dry clothes by the time the others came, and gave them cocoa.

As we rolled into our blankets, I heard Jill say, 'That's another two loads,' and Ann nudged me.

Breakfast next day was lunch as well. We had baked beans on toast.

'Whose launch was it?' Derek asked.

'A Jap patrol boat,' said Jill.

'How do they know we're up here?'

'They don't. They're just patrolling the river.'

'The Wheelers wouldn't have a searchlight that strong,' said Graham. 'In any case it was a much bigger boat than theirs.'

'Are we going back for more?' I asked.

'They didn't catch us last night,' said Jill, 'and now we know, we can dodge them. We'll take sacks and hang them along the side of the dinghy to hide it.'

'We'll use mangrove branches,' said Graham. 'To camouflage the boats. We'd look just like islands.'

'Good!' said Jill. 'We'll go again tonight. Jimmy, you and Derek clean up the camp. The rest of us'll bring up everything.'

We stacked the cases, tins, and sacks under the cliff, covering them with tarpaulins. The hermit must have picked up every old sail and scrap of canvas that floated up the river.

'I suppose he fossicked along the beaches,' said Graham.

'A beachcomber!' said Ann.

In the afternoon, we gorged on plums and peaches and slept again in the sun-dappled shade of the orchard.

Ann shook me awake. They were all sitting up and looking at me.

'It's all right,' Ann was saying.

'George was having a nightmare,' said Jimmy.

'A daymare!' said Derek. 'He's crying.'

'I just went to sleep in the sun,' I said.

As we walked back, Ann said, 'It was the hermit wasn't it?'

I nodded.

'It'll be all right now,' she said. 'I knew you'd dream about him,' and I felt better.

We made several trips to Mangrove Island, then the tides were no good, and we started having to go earlier. One morning, we crossed in daylight, but had only got to the side of the island, when we heard a boat and hid in the channel on our side. We left our boats there, crossed the island, along the crocodile's tail, and hoisted Jimmy on the blackbacks' look-out. He said a grey boat was disappearing upstream.

'Not Wheelers'?' said Graham.

'No. It's sort of like a navy boat.'

Jill nodded. 'Japs!' she said.

The hut was almost cleaned out. We'd come back for a couple of flounder spears, some empty kerosene tins, sacks, odds and ends, and vegetables, but most of all to hide any tracks we'd missed in the dark on our last visit.

Ann and I followed the boys back to the boats, sweeping out our tracks as we backed away. Jill and Graham were to follow us, making doubly sure. We were lucky Jill was so thorough.

The four of us had just dumped our loads into the boat, when there was a tremendous bang, and seagulls flew squawking over the island. We got in the dinghy and waited.

Jill and Graham had made sure there was nothing left in the hut, and they were backing away past the garden, sweeping out any last signs, when they heard the rifle shot, because that's what it was. They slid down into the mangroves, leaving as little sign as possible, and waited.

'We had to kneel in the water,' Jill told us, when they got back.

'We could see uniforms through the trees.'

'Japs!' said Jimmy.

'Who else would they be?' said Graham. 'They must have dropped back down the river with their motor idling, and sent their dinghy up the hermit's channel.'

'How do you know it wasn't the Wheelers?' asked Ann.

'Would conchies wear uniforms and fire rifles?'

'Why would the Japs fire their guns?'

'Signals,' said Graham. As he spoke, there were shouts. The soldiers must have crossed the island and seemed to be looking out from the blackbacks' roost. Thank goodness we'd cleared away all our tracks. A high shout came from further up the island.

'Sounds like Japanese,' Jill whispered.

There was another shot, a pause; another, another pause; and a third shot. We sat in the boats, silent, and heard a heavy motor come down our side of the island. Off the mouth of our channel, it slowed down. We could hear voices.

'Let's hide!' Jimmy said. He looked about to burst into tears.

'You keep still!' Jill whispered angrily.

There was a long silence, then we heard the motor further downstream.

'Let's all get in the dinghy and row across!' Jimmy said.

'Be quiet!' we all hissed at him, and Jill said very quietly, 'We'd be rowing against the tide. They'd catch us easily. Just shut up and keep still. There may be some soldiers still on the island.'

The afternoon passed slowly. We tried sleeping, and that helped. We were in the shade of a big mangrove, and pulled a tarpaulin over the dinghy, so it didn't show through the branches.

Jill and Graham crept off and checked on the shags and blackbacks. They were on their roosts, they said. Jimmy wanted to go again.

'We're not stirring till after dark,' Jill said, but she did let us out of the boats. We sat on a dried-out strip of mud and played noughts and crosses. Ann even drew a snakes and ladders game, but it got rubbed out too quickly. Then Jimmy and Derek started making a town with roads and cars made out of sticks and mangrove berries, and that kept them quiet for ages. It was very hot.

Just as a cool breeze fingered through the mangrove leaves, a lick of water came across the mud, pushing a line of dirty froth ahead. Ann looked at me and sighed. The tide had turned!

We started building a wall to hold back the water, and Jimmy and Derek got busy helping us. We were very muddy by evening.

When it was properly dark, and Jill refused to move until it was, we followed the punt up the river, going quickly with the tide. The boats seemed to fly up the creek.

None of us wanted to go far from camp next day, not even to the orchard. We took care not to make much smoke and lay around eating and talking about a bigger camp, one big enough to hold us and everything we'd salvaged from the hermit's hut on Mangrove Island.

'We beat those old Japs, didn't we!' Jimmy said.

'We haven't beaten them yet,' said Jill, but she was smiling to herself, and we all felt good, as if we'd done something clever.

CHAPTER NINETEEN
Building a Pātaka

I COULD HEAR GRAHAM WHISPERING something and getting up. Jill was moving around. It was still dark.

'Are the Japs here?' asked Jimmy.

'No, the Japs aren't here!' Jill snapped.

'I heard it too,' said Ann.

Graham must have moved suddenly. It sounded as if he were hitting something. 'I got it!' he yelled. Jill jumped out, and they thumped around.

'There goes another!' Jill shouted.

She lit the fire, and the sudden blaze of tea-tree twigs showed Graham by the stack of stores. 'I'll put the bread in the camp oven,' Jill said.

'Go back to sleep,' she told Jimmy. 'We'll have to build a storehouse tomorrow,' she told Graham, 'out of reach of the rats.'

I grinned and heard Ann laughing to herself.

'It's not funny,' Jill said. 'They could destroy everything.'

Next morning we had to throw out some bread because the rats had chewed it. 'That's what I meant last night,' said Jill.

'Are we building a storehouse?' Jimmy asked. 'On long legs?'

'A pātaka!' said Ann.

'I don't know,' Jill said. 'I suppose so. I'll have to draw a plan.'

We had two axes now, a long-handled slasher, and a couple of tomahawks. Graham marked several tall tea-tree, and we chopped them down and dragged them to the camp. Their sharp smell was good.

'How does he know which ones he'll need?' I asked Ann.

'Oh, he just knows,' she said.

Jill was checking the other stores for rat damage and

didn't want Graham to start building yet, but he began digging two holes, and we helped. We had to lie down and lift the dirt out with our hands, as the holes got deeper. Then we came to a layer of shells and ashes.

'Does that mean the sea used to come up to here?' asked Derek.

'I think it means people lived here in the olden days,' said Ann, and before Graham slid the posts into their holes, she dropped a live pipi in each. 'For the old people,' she said. Graham grunted and jiggled the posts until the forks on their tops were lined up, and we shovelled back the dirt.

'It's got to be packed really hard,' said Graham, and we rammed it down with short poles till the posts stood straight and solid. We dug four holes for the short, thick posts at the corners of the storehouse. Our hands were getting blisters. Graham had to do most of the ramming.

We laid thick poles in their forks and lashed others across to make a floor. It took all morning, and we had to drag down more of the poles we'd cut, but, by lunch-time, we had a platform that Ann and I could just see over. Jimmy and Derek had to jump up and down. It was strong and didn't move when we walked on it.

'Jill's giving Graham a telling-off for not listening,' said Jimmy, as we went up to drag down the big ridge-pole. 'She reckons Graham didn't ask her, and she had a plan for a storehouse.' But when Graham came up and helped us, he looked as if he was enjoying himself. By the platform, he looked at the posts, looked at the pole, and chopped a couple of feet off its thick end.

'Give us a hand,' he said. 'It's going to be heavy.'

We got it on to the platform and lifted one end, pointing it at the fork. 'Quick!' Graham said, glancing down. I grabbed the forked stick there, and shoved it under the ridge-pole.

'Got it?' Graham said. 'Right. Have a rest!'

Jill was doing something down at the boats. She looked up, but didn't come and help. I was balancing the ridge-pole.

124

We heaved again, got the pole into that fork, and heaved and pushed it into the other. It fell into place, tight and snug.

Graham had a tarpaulin, eyeleted and roped all around, and we spread it along the ridge-pole. He shoved me up, and I tied the ends, stretching it tight. I slid down, and we lashed the sides to the platform, so it was like a tent with its floor up in the air. We scrambled up and tried lying down inside.

Jill came then. 'Everybody give a hand', she said, 'and we'll stick the food in the storehouse.'

'Pātaka!' said Ann.

We made two long stacks with a space down the middle, so we could reach anything quickly. The tarpaulin was longer than the platform, so it stuck out and protected it, but Graham made a framework for the clearing end. 'Sew sacks over that,' he said, 'and no rain'll get in.' The open end was protected by the cliff.

Jill said, after lunch, 'Now we need to start thinking of a proper camp.'

'I suppose so,' said Graham.

'Don't just start building it though. It won't be as simple as the storehouse. We'll need two bedrooms, as well as a kitchen.'

'What for?' I asked.

'So Ann and I can have a room to ourselves.'

'Why?'

'Because we're girls!'

They talked about the new camp that night, or Jill talked and drew on the ground in front of the fire. Graham just grunted occasionally, and, once, he took a stick and drew something, but Jill said, 'No, not like that!' She was very definite about what she wanted.

Ann looked at me and grinned.

The next day was overcast. Summer seemed to have disappeared, and we wondered if we'd have another storm.

Jimmy had wet his bed again. He'd done it several times, but it didn't matter on fine days when we could just wash things out and dry them in the sun. We all wore shorts and shirts and went to bed in them, so Jimmy had to put on his spare shorts, wash out the wet ones, and the sack he lay on, and dry them in front of the fire.

'You're a confounded nuisance,' Jill said. 'You can bring in some extra firewood.'

'We can bring it up in the punt,' said Ann. 'Dead mangrove. It's good for baking.'

'I need the punt,' said Jill. 'I want the net set tonight. We should be getting some more fish smoked before the rain.'

'We can set the net and bring home a load of firewood too,' said Ann.

Jill wasn't happy about it. I suppose she thought Graham, and now Ann, were questioning her leadership.

It started raining that morning. We liked it at first. The big drops spicked all over the pool. There was no wind, and we were sheltered under the cliff. Jill and Graham got a couple of the hermit's sacking needles, split open some sugar-bags, and sewed them over the frame at the clearing end of the pātaka.

Ann and I lay underneath, watching the rain. She looked up and called to Graham, 'Won't the rats run up the legs?'

'Of course not!' Jill said.

'I've worked out something for that,' said Graham. He came down, split some of the empty kerosene tins, nailed them around the legs of the pātaka and the two posts, and bent out their tops, so they stuck out in a shining frill that would stop any rat.

'I'll make a ladder,' he said, 'and we'll all have to remember to pull it away after using it.'

'What if we didn't have nails?' I asked him.

'Chop holes in the tins and poke the legs through.'

'What if you didn't have tins?'

'Chop holes in slabs of wood and slide them up the legs.' He laughed. 'No trouble!' He could see it all in his head, I suppose.

The rain got heavier. It churned the surface of the pool and danced on the grass. Ann and I made ourselves capes out of sacks, pushing one corner inside the other and putting them over our heads so they kept us dry. We chopped and dug a channel around the tent, and the water filled it and ran down to the pool. The cliff kept the fire dry, with just a few hisses now and then.

'Ann,' said Jill, 'you and George can make some bread.'

'Good,' Ann said. 'It'll be easier with the camp oven.'

Jill began to say something and stopped. I thought she was going to say she needed the camp oven for something else.

'We can make a decent-sized loaf,' Ann went on, 'that'll keep us going a while.'

Jimmy's shorts and sack hung in front of the fire. We shifted them to one side.

'They've got to dry,' he said.

'We'll dry them faster', said Ann, 'once we've built up the fire.'

'If you'd stop being a baby,' said Jill, 'they wouldn't need drying.'

She and Graham put sack capes over their heads and went up to drag down some more firewood. Derek followed them, but Jimmy stayed with us, turning his shorts to dry.

I was kneading the dough in a tin basin. I always liked it when it got puffy and almost sprang out where I'd stuck my fingers into it.

'Give us a bit,' said Jimmy.

'You wouldn't like it.'

'Aw, go on!'

'It's dough, for bread, not cake.'

'Mum always lets me lick out the bowl,' Jimmy said. His face screwed up. He cried.

'Here!' Ann said. She pulled off a bit, dipped it in the hermit's sugar tin, and gave it to him. 'Try this.'

Jimmy stuck it in his mouth, so he stopped crying, but tears still ran down his face. He sat there sucking at the sugar and munching the dough. Ann licked her hanky and wiped his face. 'There,' she said, 'doesn't that taste good,' and Jimmy nodded, sniffed, and turned his face into her.

Suddenly, I noticed I was missing Mum too. Ann was

still holding Jimmy. 'Not you too,' she said, without turning around, and I punched the dough, flattened it around the side of the basin, and rolled it back into one big lump. A fat tear plopped off my chin and into the dough.

'It'll go sticky, and you'll have to add more flour,' she said, and I grinned and sniffed all at once.

Ann gave Jimmy a knob of fat to grease the inside of the camp oven, I put the dough in, and Ann lifted it in front of the fire.

'It's a weight!' she said. 'Don't bump it now, or it'll go down.'

Derek came back with some wood and sat by Jimmy. 'You can lift the lid and look at it rising,' said Ann, 'but be careful. If you bang the oven, it'll go down.'

We put on our capes and went for some wood. My hands were rubbed clean by the dough, and it was white under my nails. We heard the lid clang as we dragged down a log. 'That's flattened it!' Ann laughed. We chased them away, kneaded the dough again, and set it back to rise. 'You'd best leave it alone,' Ann said. 'Jill will be furious if we waste all that flour.'

It rose well the second time. We hung the oven on a hook, shovelled coals on top of the lid, and stood back, sweating. Ann tried her hand under the oven. She counted ten. 'That's hot enough,' she said. 'Now, keep away till it's done.'

The rain had almost stopped. We all dragged down more firewood, tea-tree mostly. Graham and Jill were chopping at a log. There was the sound of their axes, and the water dripping from leaf to leaf, and branch to branch.

'Look at this!' Ann said. 'George!' I pushed through some wet branches. She stood in a clearing so small we might never have found it, looking down.

CHAPTER TWENTY
The White Feather

ANN WAS LOOKING AT THREE graves on the little clearing. They were outlined by rocks from the creek, and each had a slab of timber at its head. If names had been carved there, we could not read them now.

'Look!' Ann said. 'A mother, a father, a child, and a baby.' She moved, and I saw a fourth tiny grave.

'Somebody was left,' I said. 'Somebody buried them.'

'I didn't think of that,' Ann said. 'It's a sad thought.'

Jimmy and Derek had followed our voices and joined us standing by the graves.

'I wonder if we'll all die here too?' said Jimmy.

'We're safe here,' Ann told him. 'The Japs don't know we're here, and we've got lots of food.'

'We could get sick,' said Jimmy, 'and Mum's not here to make us better.'

'We've got Graham and Jill,' Ann said. 'They're nearly grown-ups.'

We left them there and got Graham and Jill. Ann told them Jimmy was missing Mum.

'He'll be all right,' Jill said, dropping her axe. 'What about your bread: won't it be cooked?'

Ann looked at me. 'I forgot it!' she said, and she giggled and I giggled as we ran. We nearly dropped the camp oven, getting it down, but swept off the ashes and got the lid off without doing anything silly, even though we were still laughing.

The loaf was rich brown and smelled wonderful. 'What about your bread?' Ann said. 'Won't it be cooked?' and we both shrieked till she was almost crying. She sat, and I got the fire going again and hung a billy to boil. Ann just sat and stared into the fire.

'What if it happened to us?' she said, and brushed me away.

When the others came back, we had slabs of fresh bread smothered with the hermit's honey, and mugs of tea ready for them. Jill looked as if she expected the bread to be burnt. We looked at each other, and Ann went outside, but the rain drove her back.

We sat around the fire, sheltered by the cliff. Jimmy was cheerful now and wanted to go for a swim in the rain. Ann had turned his sack around, and his shorts were dry. Fresh bread always makes things better.

Jill kept talking about the sort of camp she thought we needed. She scratched away in the ashes, drawing a central part with a fireplace and a table we could all sit at.

'Whoever's cooking doesn't want to keep tripping over the rest of us sitting in front of the fire,' she said.

Graham nodded. 'Maybe we need two fires,' he said. 'One just for cooking.'

'Too much wood,' said Jill.

'Or a fireplace like old Mrs Cross's. You know, with seats inside the chimney. Then nobody'd get in your way.'

'It'd be too hot,' said Jill.

'Then you sit somewhere else,' said Graham. 'But it wouldn't be too hot in winter. That's when ingle-benches would pay off.'

'We'll have to dry clothes and sacks too,' said Jill. 'Maybe two fireplaces might be a good idea after all.'

'We can build a clothes rack,' said Graham. 'One that pulls up over your head. It'd be easy.'

'It'd need a high roof.'

'That's easy.'

Jill had an objection to everything Graham suggested. She was getting control again, and Graham liked the idea of building, so he didn't mind being bossed. They were crouched over the drawings in the ashes, when Jimmy spoke.

'Are we still going to be here in the winter?'

'Of course,' Jill said, not turning.

'What about school?'

'What school? There won't be any, not if the Japs are here. How about this?' she said to Graham.

Jimmy began crying. Jill went on drawing in the ashes. At last she noticed. 'What's the matter now?' she asked.

'I want Mum!' Jimmy sobbed, but Jill turned back to her plans, and it was Ann who comforted him. She knew he was afraid of the graves, and the hermit, and the Japs.

It was just drizzling when Graham took Ann and me to set the net. Jill said she'd cook dinner and do some more planning. We stretched the net across the creek down near the river, one end tied to a mangrove, the other to a stake that Graham drove into the soft mud.

'You could sink over your head in this stuff,' he said. 'It'd probably be better out in the river, but nobody'll see it in here.'

It was raining again and almost dark when we got back. Jill was still on about the new camp, and Jimmy was even more miserable.

'I've been thinking about the bedrooms,' Jill said. 'See, they could go off opposite ends.'

'I think we should all sleep together, like we do now,' said Jimmy. 'Then Mum could read to all of us, when we go to bed, if she was here.'

'I'll read to you,' said Ann.

'What?'

'I brought a couple of books.'

'You didn't ask me!' Jill said.

Ann ignored her. 'I knew we'd need some,' she said. 'I brought the ones George and I got for Christmas. Get under your blankets, and I'll read to you.'

Jimmy and Derek curled up between us. There was enough light from the fire for her to read from where I'd got up to, the bit about Sir Grenvile grinding glasses between his teeth and swallowing them.

'That'd kill you!' Jill said from beside the fire. 'Don't any of you try doing that.'

'Go on,' Jimmy said. 'Read us some more.' I don't know if he understood the story, but he listened.

'There! Do you see it? The bird! — the bird with the white breast!'

Each looked at the other; but Leigh, who was a quick-witted man, and an old courtier, forced a laugh instantly, and cried —

'Nonsense, brave Jack Oxenham! Leave white birds for men who will show the white feather. Mrs Leigh waits to pledge you.'

'Dad got a white feather,' said Derek.

'What's a white feather?' Jimmy asked.

'It's what you give to cowards,' said Jill. 'You give them to men who won't join up. Nobody had to give one to Dad.'

'Our father's not a coward,' said Derek. 'He was in the Great War. He got wounded twice, and he got a whole lot of medals.'

'Whoever gave him the white feather didn't know that,' said Graham.

'What'd Uncle Paul do?' Jimmy asked drowsily.

'Just showed it to us and laughed,' said Graham. 'He threw it in the fire.'

'It stunk!' said Derek.

'Who gave it to him?'

A woman in Queen Street. She pushed it into his hand and ran off in the crowd. She was a coward, he said.'

Jill coughed.

'Read some more,' Jimmy said, almost asleep. Ann read on. Outside, the rain fell steadily, and the fire hissed and burned on.

'It's a hard book to read,' Ann said. I realized she'd stopped. 'But it's put Jimmy to sleep. George!' she said. 'Are you awake?' I mumbled something, and she whispered goodnight.

The book put us all to sleep, but it didn't stop Jimmy from waking with a yell during the night, and he'd wet himself again next morning.

CHAPTER TWENTY-ONE
Oysters and a Zero

IT WAS STILL RAINING NEXT morning, but Jill had us up early. She wanted the net lifted before it was too light, just in case someone saw us, and even though it was inside the mangroves. We left her growling at Jimmy.

'It's because you didn't go before you went to bed!'

'I did so!' he cried. 'I went just before Ann read to us.'

'Well, no more reading till you stop it.'

'Come on,' Graham said, and we trotted down to the punt under our capes.

The net sagged towards the river. Graham undid one end, and we dragged it across and up the other side, slipping and sliding in the mud. The net had been busy all night, catching sticks, mangrove berries, leaves, twigs, all the rubbish the rain had brought down.

'It's going to take hours to clean it,' I said, and the rain poured on us. Then we saw the middle of the net was full of flapping flounder, big dark-backed ones, the sort that come up among the mangroves. A few got out, as we pulled the net up the mud wall of the channel, but we still had more than twenty.

'We'll smoke them,' said Graham. 'The others were all right.'

We just heaped the net in without cleaning it, had a quick look at the river for Japs, and headed home. Ann and I poled the punt while Graham knelt on the net and cleaned the flatties on a plank across the stern.

'Don't take out the roes!' I said.

'Do you think I haven't cleaned flatties before?' He turned, looked, and laughed at me. We all looked at each other and laughed. We were covered with mud and wet through.

The others had a big fire going, Jimmy's shorts and

sack hanging beside it. Jill put on both frying pan and camp oven, when she saw what we were carrying. While the flatties spat and fried, we jumped in the pool in our muddy clothes and made the water even browner. By the time we'd dressed in dry clothes, the flounder were ready.

Ann sat by Jimmy, who was all red-eyed, and gave him her roe, and I gave him mine too. We each had a piece of toast with hermit's honey, and a mug of tea. The rain pelted down, but the wall of the cliff was dry. We were warm and full of food we'd caught ourselves. It felt good.

Then Jill brought out my book. Inside the back cover, using a bit of charcoal from the fire, she'd drawn a plan of the camp she wanted.

'You might have asked if you could use my book!' I said, and she ignored me.

She'd drawn the camp standing on the clearing. There was her kitchen separating the girls' bedroom and the boys' bunkroom, there was an ordinary chimney, a table, and shelves for the stores.

'What if a plane came over?' Ann asked. 'Wouldn't they see it right away?'

Jill had forgotten about that, so she said, 'What about the storehouse?'

'It disappears under the cliff at this end,' said Graham. 'That's how it would look from a plane, part of the cliff, and I've worked out how to hide it with a tea-tree screen. It'd be harder to hide a big camp out on the middle of the clearing.'

'Well,' said Jill, 'we're not going to go on living under the cliff like a lot of savages in a cave.'

'I like being a savage!' said Jimmy and capered around with Derek.

Jill could see nobody liked her plan, and Graham wasn't going to build it. When she ordered us to clean out the net, Ann said, 'We'll get wet through again. There's nowhere to dry our clothes as it is. If we get these wet, we'll have to wear blankets.'

'You should have thought of that and cleaned out the net before you came home,' said Jill.

'There'd be more room to dry things if it weren't for Jimmy,' she said. 'You're a thorough-going nuisance!' she told him. 'I wish you'd stop being a baby and grow up.'

'I'm not a baby!'

'Look,' Ann said, 'your shorts are almost dry. I'll just turn them around. We've plenty of sacks, so this one doesn't have to be dried right now. There'll be more room for our clothes.'

When the rain eased, we all cleaned the net. It was easier. A couple of crabs had got themselves tangled and had chewed holes. One grabbed Derek, just as I warned him, in the top of his finger. He screeched, and Graham had to catch him and break off the claw, because the pincers wouldn't let go. Even then, Graham had to dig out the pincers with the tip of his knife. Derek really bawled.

After that, Jill smashed all the other crabs with a stick, and we picked them out of the net in bits. 'If you got enough crabs,' said Jill, 'you could cook the big claws off them. They'd be all right.'

'I'd like a feed of crayfish,' said Graham, 'but we won't get any up here.'

'We could set the net at night, out on the river,' said Jill. 'But we'd have to pick it up again before daylight. We might get some snapper, and there'd be big mullet too.'

We had the net cleaned and back in the punt by the time the rain started again. The rest of the day we spent drying our clothes in front of the fire, and listening to Ann reading *Westward Ho!* Graham rigged up a framework that took more clothes. By evening we could start drying our sacks, and Ann made sure Jimmy had a dry one for the night.

Then Graham said, 'I'm building the camp against the cliff.'

'I thought we'd all agreed to build my plan,' said Jill.

'It still gives us one dry wall and half a roof,' said Graham. 'I know a way we can make a proper camp for winter, against the cliff. It'll be stronger; it'll be warmer; and it'll camouflage itself so a plane won't notice it.'

Graham saw things in his mind. Jill didn't think like that; she had to have a plan she could see and touch. I did too, so I could sympathize with her, but I could understand the way Graham thought. It was just different. The trouble was Jill wanted to be boss. Graham didn't; he just wanted to build things, that's all, the way he saw them in his head.

Ann was reading to us that night when we heard a long rumble. Down the river, somewhere out over the sea, there was a flash.

'Lightning!' said Ann.

'Big guns!' said Jill.

The rumble came again. 'It could be thunder,' said Graham, but he agreed with Jill that it should have moved away after a while.

'It's guns,' she said. 'A battle out at sea. Maybe the Japs are shelling the Bay.'

'Who'd be on our side, if it was a battle?' asked Derek.

'Our Navy,' said Jill.

'They got sunk,' said Derek. 'The *Achilles* got sunk, didn't it?'

'Damaged,' said Graham. 'And the *Leander,* and the *Ajax.* But they beat the *Graf Spee.* The *Achilles* came into Auckland, remember.'

'Maybe we've got some more ships,' said Jill. 'Maybe the Americans have come.'

We were outside now, looking at the flashes. There was still banging and flashes when we went to sleep. Morning brought rain and real thunder overhead.

'Great guns do that,' said Jill. 'It always rains after a battle.'

It was too wet to do much outside. Graham chopped poles to certain lengths, working under the cliff, and he got us to carry a lot of rocks from the creek between showers, but most of the time we could only sit around, hoping the rain would stop. Jimmy's shorts steamed by the fire, and the flounder smoked browner. It was a long day.

'What if it never stops raining?' asked Jimmy.

136

'Stop moaning,' said Jill.

'It's rained all the holidays,' said Jimmy.

'It has been wet this year,' said Ann, before Jill could tell him to shut up. 'It's usually finer, so it'll clear up tomorrow.'

It stopped for a while before evening, and Graham went out and drove some stakes into the ground near the chimney. I wondered if he was going to build a bigger camp over the top of the present one.

As we ate flounder for breakfast next morning, Jimmy said, 'I wish we had some meat for a change.'

'Lots of people would give their eye teeth to swap places with you,' said Jill. 'Do you ever wonder what Dad's getting for breakfast?' But later she said, 'Let's go down and get some pipis while it's fine, and we'll see if we can't get enough oysters for a decent feed.'

The others sneaked out to get pipis, while Ann and I took Jimmy and looked for oysters. We slithered through the muddy channels, we slid and squelched when the mud was soft, we skated across where it was firm. Our legs got specked, then spotted, then smeared, then covered with mud. Jimmy got stuck, getting up the steep side of a channel, slipped, and rolled. We pulled him out, but we laughed at him, at the mud on his face and in his hair, and he laughed back.

We found a few oysters, big ones, but not as many as we wanted. The others had loads of pipis, so they dumped them in the punt and joined us downstream among the mangroves.

Graham and Jill were ahead, and we were searching around a little island of glittering white shells, reeds, and a few logs, when he whistled. He was waving us down! We lay, but he threw himself flat in the mud.

'He's lying in the mud!' said Jimmy, and a plane swept over so low it shook us.

I didn't move my head, just looked into the shells my nose rested on. A tiny crab pulled itself out of sight, emerged, and scuttled under another shell. I was just pulling out the shell when Graham yelled, 'Keep down!'

and the plane boomed again, out over the river this time, and swung left, over Whalers Beach. Its noise rolled back to us.

'Was it one of ours?' Ann asked. I shrugged.

'What sort was it?' asked Graham, running back. We were all looking at the mud down his front and on his face.

'Here!' Jill yelled from the other side of the island.

We turned and ran. She was pointing at something in the mud. There was exactly the print of a foot — toes, heel, and every part of a foot, then another, and another. A long line of footprints went across the mud where somebody had gone up into the mangroves and down again. They weren't as fresh as ours, because the tide had been over them.

We turned and ran to the nearest mangroves, scared by the plane and the footprints. Jill gathered us together there, shouting to make us listen, then holding us in a bunch. 'Keep under the branches,' she said, 'and don't look up, if it comes back.

'Derek, you listen for it, and the rest of you sit down and be quiet. I'm going to see where those tracks went.'

'Did you see the plane?' Graham asked. 'What was it? I didn't get a chance to look at it.'

'It looked like a Zero to me,' Jill said. 'I thought I saw the Rising Sun on its side.' We were silent while she was gone, sitting still in the mud.

Later, she said the tracks just went up into the scrub and came down again. She'd seen the mark where a boat had been pulled up on the edge of the mud. As she led us back through the mangroves, in case the plane came back, Graham said, 'Are you sure it was a Zero?'

'It looked like it,' Jill said. 'That's all.'

It was harder crossing the channel among the mangroves. Graham sank to his waist in the mud and had to flounder back to us, as if swimming through it. We might have laughed at him, covered in mud, but he was clearly frightened.

'Don't any of you try crossing the channels on your

own,' he said. 'I could feel it sucking me down like quicksand.' Jill found a firmer crossing, and he washed some of the mud off his face.

It was as we headed back through the mangroves that we found the oysters, thousands of them crusted on roots and rocks. We knocked them off and filled our pīkaus. We got back to the punt nearly as muddy as Graham.

Jill had found an oyster opener at the hermit's, a screwdriver driven through a block of wood. She just put the lip of the oyster over the edge of the screwdriver, gave a tap, and the shell came off. Derek and Jimmy spooned them into a billy. 'Oyster fritters!' Jill said when the billy was nearly half full.

'How do the Japs know we're here?' asked Jimmy.

'I don't know,' said Jill, 'but they do seem to be looking for us. Perhaps we should dig some slit trenches by the camp.

'Come on!' she said. 'Let's light the fire and have some fritters.'

'Won't they see our smoke?'

'It's clouding over,' she said. In fact it was starting to rain. 'Most of the smoke disappears up the cliff and into the bush anyway.'

Jill seemed excited by the plane, pleased it had come. We lit the fire, mixed a batter, and stirred in the oysters. We sat in a circle and filled ourselves with fritters, brown, crumbly, and packed with juicy oysters.

CHAPTER TWENTY-TWO
The Empty Grave

'I'M GOING OUT TO MANGROVE Island,' Jill said that night. 'Graham and I'll go. Maybe somebody's living in the hermit's hut, maybe the person who left those tracks.

'I've got to find out. It's no good us being afraid of them. We'd be better to know who it is.'

'What if it's the Japs?' Derek asked.

'They're not likely to be living in the hermit's hut,' said Jill. 'No, it's more likely somebody hiding from them, like us.'

'Do you think it's Mum and Aunty Iris?' asked Jimmy.

'No, they wouldn't leave the bach in case we came back. We've got to find who it is though, because they could lead the Japs to us.

'We've got to take more care, put that boom across the creek. We might even have to shift camp.'

'I don't want to leave here,' said Jimmy. 'I like it.'

The tide was well in when Graham and Jill left, and it was very late. 'One thing about Jill,' Ann said, as they vanished down the creek, 'she's brave!'

Jimmy and Derek wanted Ann to read to them, but fell asleep as soon as she'd begun. We must have slept soon after. I woke once, and they weren't back. They weren't back next morning either.

'The Japs have caught them,' Jimmy said.

We went down the creek as far as the mangrove hedge. The river was empty, and Mangrove Island looked deserted, no smoke, no signal. We went back to camp wondering what to do.

The boys got a basket of peaches, and we tried making a pie. We'd had a feed of smoked flounder and mashed potatoes, so the pie was just for filling their hollow legs, I told Jimmy and Derek. Ann tapped their knees and said she could hear echoes, and they laughed, but they were worried about Graham and Jill.

Towards evening, we took sacks to keep us warm and rowed down the creek. The tide was still out, and we waited a long time for it to get dark. We kept to the edge, then rowed fast to the island and hid the dinghy up the channel on our side. Jimmy and Derek got in their sacks, and we pushed them under a log on the shelly ridge. 'Don't move', I said, 'till we come back.'

'We'll call your names,' said Ann, 'so you'll know it's us,' and we crept away through the gloom, trying not to crunch the shells.

We crept up on the hut, paused, counted five hundred, and crept again. We crept and listened again. Ann touched me, and we crawled around the back. There was no sound inside. It felt empty.

I stole inside, listening for somebody breathing, but there was nobody on the bunk nor in the chair. Ann joined me, as I struck a match.

'The punt's not there,' she said. I was pleased she'd gone down, because I didn't want to go past the hermit's grave on my own, but she led me out of the hut and down the track.

'Look!' she said. The hairs stood up on the back of my neck. I could feel them. The hermit's grave was empty. It was open and black. I clutched Ann, then far away out on the island there arose, all of a sudden, a sound like a cry of anger, then another on the back of it; and then one horrid long-drawn scream.

Through the dark, we ran back to Jimmy and Derek and away from the open grave. They were screaming for us. We heard more shrieks, then we were there. Graham and Jill were there. Jimmy and Derek were there. It was all right, but we were all crying and laughing.

Graham and Jill had been looking for us. They'd come up the channel, found the dinghy, and set out along the shelly ridge. They didn't know Jimmy and Derek were snuggled under the log in their sacks.

Jimmy and Derek heard them coming, but knew it

couldn't be us, because we'd gone the other way. They listened to their splashing and, when their two dark forms crept up the sandbank, bending over and looking for our tracks in the dark, Derek said, 'Crocodiles!' to Jimmy, and they scrambled off, hooded under their sacks. Jill and Graham were almost standing on top of them. They screamed with fright, and Jimmy and Derek joined in.

'You screamed first!' we said to Jill and Graham, and we all shrieked with laughter. We laughed, we yelled, we jumped up and down, and Jimmy first, then Derek, began to cry.

'Come on,' we said, and got them into their sacks and piggy-backed them down to the dinghy, where they cheered up.

'Sound travels!' said Jill, and suddenly that was funny, and Jimmy repeated, 'Sound travels!' and we all laughed again. Every time Jill quietened us, we'd burst out again.

It was the first time for ages we'd all laughed together. We laughed all the way across the river, through the mangroves, and up the creek home. If the Japs had been out on the river that night, they must have caught us.

Wrapped in our blankets, sipping boiling-hot cocoa, we sat and listened to Jill's story. The flames lit our faces and the cliff above. Jimmy and Derek squashed between Ann and me. Everything was safe.

'We rowed across in the dark, down this side of the island,' Jill said. 'We slid the punt through the mangroves and across the mud. It took ages because we were so quiet.

'There was nobody in the hut. We made sure of that. Then Graham found the hermit's grave was open.'

'We saw it!' I said. 'Just as you all screamed. We were standing there looking down into the darkness, and I remembered the ghost in the picture we saw at the Bay last year, remember the one who dug himself out of his grave?'

'I'd felt with a stick', said Ann, 'and knew he wasn't still in there, but didn't have time to tell George.'

'The Japs must've dug him up,' said Jill. 'Anyway, we searched around the island and were coming back past the hut, and somebody was there. They were smoking, and we smelled it, or we'd have walked right into them.

'They lit the fire in the hut, and we could see its light. We sneaked across the garden and towards the punt in the mangroves.'

'That's where I fell over,' said Graham. 'Something moved under my foot, and I fell with a splash.'

'We thought we were caught,' said Jill. 'We could see somebody in uniform at the door of the hut, looking straight towards us. He stood and stared for ages. The light was behind him. That's what saved us.

'Then somebody called from inside, and the soldier went back. He must have thought it was a fish jumping.'

'Did they talk Japanese?' asked Derek.

'We couldn't hear.'

'We were just too far away,' said Graham.

Jill went on. 'We'd sunk in the mud. It took ages to pull ourselves out. Graham got free and helped me, then I got stuck again and almost fell over. They must have heard me splashing around, because one of them came out of the hut again and stood listening for about five minutes. It took us about an hour to get away, we had to move so slowly, and I knew the tide was going out all the time.'

'What happened?'

'We got back to the punt, but it was high and dry, miles from the water. We tried dragging it, but it was too heavy, so we gave up and sat in it the rest of the night.'

'When it got light', said Graham, 'we heard them calling each other. We thought they'd find our tracks and follow us down to the punt, so we decided to wade out through the mangroves and swim up the top end of the island. But the tide had turned and was coming across the mud. The punt lifted, and we slid deep into the mangroves where nobody could find us. We hid there the rest of the day.'

'We were scared you'd come looking for us,' said Jill.

'We looked, but we kept out of sight,' I said.

'Good! Well, Graham thought he heard a motor, so we waited, then sneaked up on the hut, and they'd gone.

We could see their tracks going down to the hermit's channel. We went back and wiped out all our own tracks.

'When it got dark, we rowed straight across the other side. Graham was sure he saw you disappearing into the mangroves over here, so we came back, found the dinghy, and walked on top of Jimmy and Derek.

'They looked like some sort of strange animals running at us in the dark. We couldn't see they were wearing sacks. They looked like hump-backed animals without any heads. That's when we yelled.'

'Sound travels!' said Jimmy, and we all laughed.

'Who was it on the island then?' I asked.

'We don't know. It's more than one person. They didn't worry about hiding the light from the fire, and they didn't try to be quiet, so I suppose they were Japs,' said Jill.

'Why'd they dig up the hermit?'

'Just to make sure he was dead, I suppose.'

Jimmy shivered. 'I wonder what they did with him?' he said, and I could feel Ann tighten her arm around him.

Book Three
GOING HOME

CHAPTER TWENTY-THREE
Chimney, Dam, and Garden

WE STUCK CLOSE TO HOME and helped Graham build a chimney for the new camp. One side of it was the cliff. The back and other side were built of rocks inside a framework to stop them collapsing. Where the rocks finished, above our heads, Graham continued it with poles, right up to the bulge of the cliff. It was a huge chimney, bigger than old Mrs Cross's, with seats along each side, and we could all sit inside it, out of the cold. There was lots of room for drying clothes, for cooking, and for smoking fish. It was a marvellous chimney.

Building the new camp didn't go as fast. There was so much Jill wanted done before winter. We were digging a garden because she reckoned we should be picking our own vegetables soon, and she wanted to plant potatoes at once. I said I remembered Dad planting potatoes later, and Mr Campbell had dug up his front lawn and planted it in potatoes last year, and that hadn't been at the end of summer. Lots of people had dug up their lawns to grow potatoes for the war effort. I tried to argue with Jill because I didn't want to have to dig the garden, but she said I was too young to know.

We had two boats, the net, spears, and lines. We had fish, oysters, pipis, and fruit. I suppose it all seemed too easy. Anyway, Jill said we needed plenty to do, or we'd be at each others' throats. She sounded like Mum being grumpy, more and more.

'What can we do to keep them busy?' I heard her say to Graham.

'The pool's not much good for swimming,' he said. 'It's not deep enough.'

'Well, we can't go swimming in the river!'

'I was thinking of damming the creek,' Graham said.

'That'd make the pool deeper.' He couldn't say how, but he knew. He had it worked out in his head.

It took us days to get all the thick tea-tree poles he wanted and to drag them down to the creek. He spent hours in the water, working out where to put the dam, trying the bottom with a shovel, poking among the rocks, and digging into the banks.

'The only trouble is how to get the stakes to stand in the middle,' he said.

'Hammer them in with an axe,' I said.

'They won't go in far enough. They've got to hold all that weight of water, and we don't want them washing out on the first flood.'

In the end we got in three stakes leaning upstream and three leaning down, so their forked tops interlocked. We worked their ends down among the rocks, so they were gripped fast. In line with them we drove interlocking stakes in the banks.

Graham laid poles across, locking them between the forks of the stakes. They held the stakes firm, and the stakes held them. Even the press of water seemed to tighten everything together. The stakes couldn't move up or down, and they couldn't move sideways.

'It'd do for a bridge,' I said.

Graham just nodded and said, 'Bit narrow.'

We put in more logs against the top stakes and weighed them down with rocks. As more logs went in, the water rose and pinned them in place. When the face was finished, we had a waterfall a couple of feet high and right across the creek. Graham kept us working till it was backed with rocks we levered out of the bottom of the pool and half carried, half swam to a gap in the middle, the spillway, he called it. He packed the rocks in behind the logs and into the banks, so the creek couldn't chew around the ends. The dam was now wide enough to walk across.

There were no rocks left in the pool, just a flat-topped boulder, almost level with the surface, that we could slide on to for sunbathing. We could touch the bottom in front of the dam, and that's where Jimmy and Derek played most of the time. At the top end, the waterfall now fell into water so deep we had to dive to touch the bottom. We spent whole days in the pool.

Jill made us work in the garden too. The hermit had kept vegetable seeds in Riverhead Gold tobacco tins, with their names scratched on the lids. We had radishes nearly ready, lettuce and cabbage plants coming up, and several rows of carrots.

Jill and Graham sneaked back to the island one night and brought back cabbages, silver beet, and several pumpkins.

'There's nobody on the island,' Jill said. 'The garden's just about finished, so we've got to get ours going faster. We might bring across some bags of soil from his garden. It's very rich.'

We ate the cabbage raw, and it was good. I'd always hated it boiled, and I knew Ann hated the smell. Jimmy wouldn't eat the silver beet or the pumpkin. He reckoned they made him sick. One night Jill told him he couldn't eat anything else till he'd eaten his pumpkin.

He just sat and looked at his plate, of course. Jill stuck another bit on his plate.

'Eat it all,' she said, 'or go to bed.'

'You're not the boss,' Jimmy said. 'You're not Mum.'

We didn't see it, but Derek told us about it later, when we came back from setting the net. Jimmy was in bed crying.

'We've got to have a system,' Jill said. 'He's got to learn to eat everything. Things won't just go on happening.'

'What do you mean?' asked Ann. She'd quietened Jimmy.

'We've been lucky, so far,' said Jill, 'but winter's coming, and food's going to be harder to get. There won't be as many fish in the river.'

'Where'll they go?' I asked.

'They move,' said Jill. 'They don't just stay there all the time. It's going to get cold, and we'll need bigger fires and more wood. Netting and spearing flatties is going to be cold work.

'We've got to get the garden going, and Jimmy's got

to learn to eat what's put in front of him, just like everybody else.'

That was when she started her job list. We all had certain duties each day. First, we had to drag down some firewood, while the person on duty cooked breakfast. If we didn't bring enough, Jill sent us up for more. Only when she was satisfied were we allowed to have breakfast.

Of course Jimmy was sent back again and again. He didn't see why he had to bring as much as the rest of us. He was smaller, he said. By now he was just against anything Jill said.

After breakfast, we had to clean up the camp. The net might have to be cleaned and stowed back in the punt. If we'd brought up a load of dead mangrove, that had to be carried up, stacked under the cliff, and the punt cleaned out. When Jimmy didn't clean it properly once, Jill wouldn't let him have any lunch.

Usually, we spent the morning in the garden. Jill reckoned you could grow a late crop of potatoes in the Bay, so we had to dig a huge garden for them.

'With six of us eating them, we're getting through the hermit's spuds,' she said. 'They'll be finished before winter.'

'How long are we staying?' said Jimmy.

'Till the Japs have gone.'

'I'm not staying that long.'

'Oh,' said Jill, 'and where are you going?'

'I'm going home.'

'How?'

'I don't know, but I'll get there.'

Jill laughed. She knew Jimmy was scared of deep water. 'You could try swimming,' she said. 'Remember the sharks we saw on the bar. And the river's full of stingarees.'

So we skimmed the turf off the clearing and dug the soil. As soon as we got a new patch dug, Jill made us put in potatoes, each one a foot apart and enough space between the rows to heap them up as they grew, the way Dad did back home.

When she was satisfied we'd done enough, we were allowed to go to the orchard. There were peaches and nectarines now, and the apples were getting ripe, but the grapes were still hard.

Graham went on slowly with the camp, not the one Jill wanted. It grew along the cliff and over the top of the old one. There was much more room, and Graham made a big table and shelves out of planks he split from a kauri log down by the river.

It was more comfortable. Cooking was easier, and drying clothes, and it was good sitting in the chimney, especially on wet nights, but Jill didn't get her separate bedroom, and we didn't build bunks.

When we were sitting in the chimney, Ann and I fenced up Jimmy with our legs so Jill couldn't reach him. We thought up all sorts of ways of keeping them apart and told Jimmy what to do, so he wouldn't annoy her and get a hiding, but we couldn't be there all the time. Every day or two, we'd come in and find him crying under his blanket, and he wet himself every night.

CHAPTER TWENTY-FOUR
The Jap Camp

IT HAD BEEN FUN, A lot of it, running away up the Mangrove River, but now it was hard work. We weren't allowed to swim most of the time and even going to the orchard became just another job on Jill's list. If we took too long, or helped ourselves to fruit, she was there telling us off, hurrying us up.

We had tried to get up the creek above the waterfall when we first came, but it was overgrown with scrub, and we soon gave up. Now, Jill was determined to try again.

'If we had a look-out,' she said, 'we could see what's going on down the river and out on the island.'

She inspected the camp one morning, the firewood stack, the garden, and the boats. 'Right,' she said, 'we're off up the creek!'

'I'm hungry,' Jimmy said. 'Are we going to have something to eat before we go?'

'George, you and Ann bring the billy,' Jill ordered. 'We'll boil up somewhere in the creek.'

Jimmy whined, and I knew he was hungry, but Jill soon had us all up the cliff and pushing through the overhanging scrub of the creek. When Graham and Jill got ahead, Ann swung off her pıkau, undid the rope, and gave Jimmy and Derek a piece of bread each and some peaches.

'Keep out of Jill's sight', she said, 'till you've finished.'

We were hungry too before Jill decided to stop and have lunch. The creek had been hard climbing the whole way, choked with scrub and one little waterfall after another. We were all scratched and itching with leaves and twigs down our necks.

'We're all scratchy,' said Ann, and I had to grin, because it was true. Jimmy and Derek were grizzling; Jill was bullying; Graham wasn't saying anything, just sulking away inside; I was fed up; even Ann was grumpy.

Where the creek split into several tiny streams, we boiled up and picked the twigs out of our shirts. 'Here,' Ann said, while I mixed the milk powder, 'sit here and eat this,' and she gave the boys some bread and smoked fish.

Graham and Jill tried to get up a couple of side streams, but came back beaten. I gave them their mugs of tea.

'There's nowhere we'll get a look at the river,' Graham said.

'We'll find a look-out', Jill said, 'if we just keep going long enough.'

'Why?' said Jimmy. 'There's been nothing so far.'

Jill scowled. Jimmy had the knack of asking the wrong question, and he was often right. Even if we found a look-out now, it was too far from camp to be any use.

When Jill got to her feet and said, 'Come on. Get moving!' Jimmy said, 'I'm not going any further.'

'You get on your feet!'

'We're too tired.' Jimmy looked at Derek. 'We don't want to go up your old creek.'

Jill looked as if she'd like to hit him, but Graham said, 'Come on, leave him alone.'

'You two go on and see if you can find anything,' said Ann. 'We'll stay with them, so they don't wander off and get lost.'

'I'll try and climb the side of the hill,' I said.

Jill snorted and crashed off with Graham behind her. They were hot and bad tempered when they came back later. We had the billy boiling, and they felt better after a mug of tea.

'There's nothing up there,' said Graham, 'nothing but miles of scrub stretching on and on. We had to give up. There's no way through it. The scrub's a solid wall, miles thick. One thing about it, nobody's going to come this way and find us.'

Jill drank her tea and said nothing. Her face was red, and scratches criss-crossed her arms and legs. Blood had dried on a cut on her neck.

'Did you climb the hill?' she asked me.

I nodded. 'I tried, but there's no way through the scrub.'

Ann said, 'He tried for ages. It's too thick.'

In fact, after they'd gone, I helped Jimmy and Derek start damming the creek, and then climbed the hill.

It was just what Graham said, a solid wall of scrub miles thick that I tried to push through, burrow under, even climb over. I couldn't get uphill against it, so worked my way across the side of the hill. I saw what looked like a more open patch, pushed through the tea-tree, and stepped on to the foot of a slip of red clay. It was a strange feeling to be standing in the open again.

I laid some fern leaves on the clay, to mark where I'd come out. The sun shimmered off the slip. It was hot climbing it, but I was in the open! From the top, I could see back down the creek and out over the islands and channels of Mangrove River, up to where it vanished and reappeared among the hills.

There was the Wheelers' farm, smooth paddocks of bright green running up into the bush. I could see the bar and the beginning of Whalers Beach. From higher, I could see the whole of Whalers Beach, and, far away, a dark line which must have been the cliffs of our creek and the bach. It was too far away to see any smoke. Between us, there were miles of scrubby hills. My throat felt sore with dryness and the dust off the scrub. I wondered if Mum and Aunty Iris were at the bach.

In the gully beneath, there was just more scrub and what was probably another creek. And away down it, there was a rubble heap with a pair of straight lines across it: the old gold mine with its rails out of the tunnel.

I crouched, just my head out of the tea-tree, watched the movement down there, and went back to the others. I didn't tell them what I'd seen, just said I couldn't get through the scrub.

Jimmy and Derek were all right for a while on the trip home, then their legs seemed to droop from their bodies, and we had to rest again and again. Ann and I kept them walking between us, so they couldn't fall behind. It took a long time to reach the camp. Ann fed them at once, and they both went to bed.

They were still tired next morning. When Jill started shouting at them to get up, I said, 'Let them sleep in. They're only little, remember.'

'I want to get things done,' Jill said. I could see she didn't want to give in. 'We had yesterday off,' she said, 'so we've got to catch up on the work.'

'The boys didn't have yesterday off,' said Ann. 'Let them sleep in, and we'll bring down their share of wood.'

'They've got to learn to pull their weight,' Jill said, but she grumbled off and left them alone.

We were carrying a kerosene tin of water from the creek to the garden, when Ann said to me, 'What did you see yesterday?'

I was used to her knowing things before I told her, so I said, 'The old gold mine with the tunnel and the rails. They were over the next hill a fair way, but I could see them.'

'Could you get there?'

'Not without slashing a track for miles.'

'Those carrots are going to need thinning! You planted them too thick.' Jill was standing over us, checking our work.

'Are you going to tell her?' Ann asked, as we went down to the creek with the empty tin.

'No,' I said. 'Let's keep it a secret. Besides, there was something else.' Ann said nothing.

'A tent,' I said. 'There was a tent where we boiled the billy that day.'

'Could you see anybody there? Maybe it was Aunty Iris and Aunty May hiding there from the Japs!'

'There were people there, but they were soldiers,' I said.

'The Mounted Rifles?'

'I didn't think of them because there weren't any horses. No, I think they must have been the Japs.'

'Did you see anything else?'

'A big ship outside the islands, and what looked like a couple of destroyers with it.'

'Japanese?'

'I suppose so.'

We tipped the tin, so the water ran betwen the rows of young lettuce and cabbage plants. Ann blocked it with her foot, so it turned amongst the carrots and disappeared into the soil.

'Keep it quiet for a while,' she said. 'Jimmy's worried enough. Do you think they'll find us?'

'Not through all that scrub,' I said.

'Come on!' Jill yelled. 'You're getting nothing done, talking all the time.'

We dug along between the rows, using the edges of the shovel and spade.

'Why would the Japs camp over at the gold mine?' And asked.

'Search me!' I said. 'I suppose they're searching the whole country for runaways.'

'Mmm. Seems funny though. I suppose it just shows Jill was right: the Japs were coming, and nobody was doing anything to stop them. We must have got away just in time.'

CHAPTER TWENTY-FIVE
Making a Kōneke

W E STILL HAD FUN SOMETIMES. Graham wasn't bossy
like Jill and never hit us. She never tried hitting him,
of course.

'Don't tell Jill,' he said, as we went down the creek one
evening. 'We'll set the net in the river, just off the pipi
bank. We might get some snapper there.'

It was dark, and we listened for the sound of a motor
before sliding the punt through the mangroves and setting
the net with buoys to mark its ends. Graham made sure
it was anchored just where he wanted it, not too shallow,
and not too deep.

As we went up the creek, we sang some songs we all
knew from the radio music book. It seemed funny, Graham
and Ann listening to the same lessons up in Auckland,
while we listened to them down home. We sang all the
way, and were tired but happy when we got back.

Graham shook us awake early. We had to feel our way
down the creek, it was so black. The seats in the punt
were wet and cold. Graham made straight for the net,
as if he could see in the dark. 'Just get it into the punt,'
he said. 'We'll sort it out back in the mangroves.'

Something shiny and silver came up in it. 'A snapper!'
Ann whispered. 'There's another,' she said, and there were
more. We pulled the net over the stern, while Graham
held us square on to the current. The sky was looking
a little grey over the other side of the river, as we slipped
back through the mangroves.

It took a while, cleaning it. The snapper had twisted
themselves around and around. A couple were eaten out
by crabs, but there were twelve good ones, shiny-red, silver-
scaled snapper with blunt heads and big eyes. There were
a few flounder, a couple of John Dory, some kahawai,
and several big mullet.

We could hear the others getting up as we returned. Jill was telling off Jimmy, and he came out snivelling, dragging his wet shorts and sack down to the creek. Jill followed, shouting.

'Hey!' Graham yelled, as she went to hit him again, and he held up a snapper.

Jill was furious. 'You set it in the river!' she said. 'I told you never to . . .' She grumbled, but there was nothing she could do to Graham. We all had a piece of John Dory and as much snapper as we liked, and we squeezed fresh lemons on them.

'Corker fish!' said Derek.

'That's because they're from the river,' said Jimmy, and Jill glared at him.

'We can survive here for ever,' said Graham. 'Fresh fish from the river, veges from the garden, fruit.'

'What about clothes?' said Ann.

'I've been thinking about that. We could pinch some sheep from the Wheelers and run them on the clearing. We could teach ourselves to spin their wool. Knitting's easy enough, but we could work out how to weave too.'

Nothing was ever a bother to Graham. He could work things out.

'There's all this flax up here,' he said. 'We could make flax ropes, and flax cloaks for the rain.'

'I'll make you a flax skirt, if you'll wear it,' Ann said, and I gave her a shove.

'That's enough fooling around,' said Jill. 'You can just be thankful you weren't caught in the river this morning. Now there's work to be done.

'Jimmy, you and Derek can get some more wood. George, you and Ann clean up the camp, hang the fish to smoke, then you can start watering the garden.'

But she didn't tell Graham what to do. He went off to where we'd dug a hole for a dunny, and, later, we saw him pushing little sticks in the ground, lying down, and measuring them with his eye. When we asked what he was doing, he said, 'Saving you some work.'

There was a boggy patch on the way to the orchard.

We always got muddy legs going through it. Graham dug a shallow channel across, and it filled slowly, as he chopped another channel through the scrub and on to the clearing.

'What's the use?' Jill said. 'You're spending ages mucking around on it, and there's other things need doing.'

'It'll save us a lot of work,' said Graham. 'Ann and George are spending hours carrying water.'

We helped. Graham made us keep the drain shallow, and it filled slowly behind us. He said that was good. Where it came across the top of the clearing, he dug several channels to the garden, brought some slabs he'd split, and we used them as water gates. It was going to be easy to water the garden.

He had another idea too. We'd burned all the handy stuff and were dragging firewood from further and further away. Jill was making a store for winter. Even when we brought up the punt filled with mangrove, it still had to be carried up to the camp.

Graham chopped the fork out of a big branch, so he had a piece shaped like a wishbone. He was chopping away where the two arms joined, shaping it so it curved up, when Ann and I joined him. He tipped it over.

'What do you think of that?'

'What is it?' I asked, and Ann said, 'I see.'

'See what?'

'Gosh, you're slow,' Ann said. 'It's a sledge!'

Graham tied a rope on the end, we all pulled, and the sledge came bumping and thumping over the roots and on to the clearing.

'Jump on!' said Graham, and we sat and hung on to each other, while he towed us, skidding across the grass to the camp, where we broadsided and rolled off at Jill's feet.

'A kōneke!' she yelled.

'Call it what you like,' said Graham, 'but it's going to make getting firewood a lot easier.'

We sledged huge loads of wood down from the bush and up from the punt. We'd tie several ropes to the front and be huskies. We barked and snarled, and Graham waved a whip and whistled, and we barked and tried to bite him. We'd stack the firewood under the cliff and take turns riding the kōneke back to the boat. Graham had nailed planks across the two arms, so it was easier to load. The Eskimos tried to ride all the way down, but the huskies always managed to tip them off.

Jill said there was no need to make such a row and complained we were making a mess of the grass, but even she had to admit we were getting a good stack ready for winter.

When she suggested Graham might bring water down past the camp, he said, 'We could, but it'd make the place damp. Besides, it's not far to the creek.'

The radishes were getting nearly big enough to eat. They were hot. The lettuce and cabbages were growing. The garden was beginning to show results.

We made lots of things for the camp, most of them Graham's ideas, like the toasting fork. We'd brought a roll of number eight wire from Mangrove Island for hooks to hang billies over the fire. Graham took a length, doubled it, and twisted it into a long handle. He bent the two ends up and down so they held a piece of bread. It was better than using forked sticks, because you didn't have to poke holes in the bread. We made several of them.

Graham wired the dam together. 'It'll be stronger,' he said. He made a billy hook out of two pieces of wire twisted together, for lifting billies and the camp oven, when their handles were hot.

We had wires across the chimney, well up, for smoking fish. Sometimes they fell off, so we made a wire rack for them. We made racks for our plates, we made handles for the four-gallon tins, we made spare spears and a couple of gaffs out of wire.

'How did people live before wire?' Ann asked

'They didn't miss it, because they didn't know about it,' I said.

She thought. 'Do you miss much?' she said.

'Not much. But I miss Mum and Aunty Iris, and I wonder what's happened to Dad.'

'I dreamt Dad was looking for us,' said Ann, 'so the Japs hadn't caught him yet.'

'He survived the Great War,' I said. 'He'll survive this one.'

'I'd just like him to know we're all right,' she said and was very quiet. I tried to comfort her, and I wished we could let everybody know we were all right: Mum, Dad, Aunty Iris, and Uncle Paul.

It was funny though, Graham didn't say much about them, and Jill never mentioned them at all. It was Jimmy and Derek who missed them most.

CHAPTER TWENTY-SIX
Killing a Stingaree

KEEP HER HEAD INTO THE wind!' Jill shouted. "It's hard enough getting the net in, without worrying about going over the side.'

Ann and I pulled the bow back into the wind. The current kept taking it around.

'Look out where you put your feet,' said Graham. 'That one could get you.'

'Here comes the other weight,' said Jill. 'Now, let's get off the river. Come on, pull!'

She and Graham half-crouched on the stern, holding on to the sides, balancing as the waves slopped towards us, lifted, and dropped. The net was a tangled mound they couldn't climb past, a twisted mass of branches, seaweed, and, flapping wildly in the middle of it, two stingrays. Graham lifted some folds of the net and dropped it over the sting, where one had flapped half free.

The wind had come up in the night, and, as we rowed down the creek, we heard thumping on the bar, and the boom of surf along Whalers Beach.

'Must be a big sea,' said Graham, 'if we can hear it right up the river.'

Jill had insisted on setting the net away out in the main channel, and we had trouble finding it in the dark. Waves were running up the river, and the fetch from the other side was long enough for the wind to build up waves inside, so there was a dangerous jobble of criss-cross chops. Even when we found the net, it was all Graham and Jill could do to get it aboard, and getting the stingrays over the stern had been exciting. We took in water several times.

'Stingarees!' said Graham. 'I wonder what the hermit did when he caught them?'

'Ate them!' said Jill. 'Come on, you two. Pull!'

It was light on the river, a nasty, grey light. Mangrove

162

Island shrugged itself out of the darkness, and the other side was a threatening gloom, as Jill yelled at us again. I looked down, kept my feet away from the stingray, and threw my weight into rowing. A wave picked us up, crashed the punt over some small mangroves, and carried us clear into our channel and out of sight. Everybody relaxed as if we had escaped some rough beast slouching towards us out on the river.

We ran on a sandbank and cleaned the net, lifting out a yard or two at a time, picking out the twigs, the sticks, and seaweed. All sorts of rubbish had been caught, even a clump of reeds.

'Grab it where the sting can't reach you,' Jill said.

'They can't do much, not with the net holding them down,' said Graham, 'but be careful. Ready. Lift!'

We swung and dragged out a section of the net where a stingray was wound and wound inside at the centre of a huge knotty tangle. It lay there, unable to move, watching us, seeming to know we were going to kill it, yet we felt no pity. It looked malevolent. As Graham and Jill lifted off a few meshes, it lifted its wings, as if to fly and come down upon us with its barbed sting.

At that, Jill beat it with the handle of an oar, and Graham stabbed it through and through the head with a spear. When, at last, it lay without heaving, he hacked through the base of the sting and lifted it away between two sticks.

'They're poisonous,' Jill said. 'If it whipped that barb into you, you'd die of poisoning.'

'It's just the slime they pick up as they swim,' said Graham. 'That's what poisons you. Robert Morehu in the Bay, he got stung diving for crays, and he didn't die. He cleaned out the stingaree's rips and made them bleed, and they healed.'

'They told us at Guides they're poisonous,' said Jill, in her flattest voice.

'Well, that's what Robert told me,' said Graham. 'He showed me the scars, all down his side.'

'If you want to believe Robert Morehu,' said Jill, 'that's all right with me. I know who I'd rather believe.'

'Whoever's right,' said Graham, 'don't stand on it,' and he put the sting away, well under the stern thwart.

'Remember that girl along the Thames coast, near Puru,' said Ann. 'She dived right on top of a stingaree in shallow water, and its sting went right through her heart. She died. Aunty Iris told us. Remember?'

Graham cut the thick wings off the dead stingaree and shoved the evil-looking hulk into the deep water of the channel and out of sight.

The other one came out easily. It was breathing and humping itself up on its wings. 'Cut off its sting!' Ann said. 'For that girl they killed!'

Graham tried to hold it down with an oar, but the stingray flapped and slid into shallow water. Its long tail whipped. The sting rose like a pointing finger. It jerked around.

Jill whacked at it with an oar. Graham jumped for the spear. The stingray flapped and showered water and mud everywhere. We staggered back.

'Kill it!' Ann shrieked. 'Kill it, George!'

We danced around with oars and the spear, but it was gone. It disappeared, shoving up a mound of water, then even that was gone. We were too scared to go after it. The two tips of its wings rose from the muddy water once, and it must have found the channel.

'Why'd you let it go?' Ann yelled at me. I stared. She was nearly crying.

We finished cleaning the net. There were no snapper, no mullet, just a couple of kahawai. 'Oh, well, we can smoke them,' said Graham. 'Hardly worth it, really.'

'At least, we saved the net,' said Jill. 'It'd have carried away, with all that stuff in it.'

'Why'd you want to kill that old stingaree?' I asked Ann. She'd got into the punt, as if scared it might be waiting in the water, as we pushed off.

'I hate them!' was all she'd say. We were silent, all the way home. Rain fell heavily and worked its way through our sacks.

There was a dull, heavy sort of light, by the time we

reached the clearing, and no welcoming smoke from the chimney. Jimmy and Derek weren't there.

'You heard me,' said Jill. 'I told them to have a fire going and breakfast ready. They didn't even leave a billy of water to heat. I'm going to have to teach them a lesson.'

'They're young,' said Ann.

'They're going to have to learn to do their share of the work,' said Jill. She'd already had a go at Jimmy that morning, before we'd left.

'They do quite a lot, in fact,' said Ann. She sounded tired. 'I'll make some porridge.'

I was lighting the fire. She knelt beside me and touched my hand, as I raked back the ashes and revealed last night's embers. The tea-tree twigs burst into flames at once. The billy boiled while we got into dry clothes. We had a mug of tea, and Ann gave us all porridge.

'You can make us some bread,' Jill said. 'We can't just have people taking off whenever it suits them.'

While we baked the bread, Graham put a dry sack over his head and went to the orchard, to see if Jimmy and Derek were there.

'No sign of them,' he said later. 'I suppose they're off in the bush, under a dry tree. They'll come back when they're hungry.'

He'd brought down some plums, big ones with red flesh. We sat in the chimney eating them and waiting for the bread to bake. The stone walls reflected the heat. We were warm and dry. The coarse flesh of the plums was rich, the red juice stained our hands and mouths. Outside, the rain was heavier, and water poured down the trench around the camp. The creek was high and brown with mud. Jill filled a couple of tins and said, 'Better let it settle, before you drink any of it.

'I'll give them both the hiding of their lives,' she said, but she sounded unconvinced, as if worried rather than angry. I remembered again she'd had Jimmy crying before we left to pick up the net. She'd hit him because he'd wet himself again, and it was going to be a wet day, and we'd have his wet things hanging in the chimney. He was crying as we went down to the punt.

'They haven't done anything terrible,' Graham said. 'Probably under a leaning tree somewhere, trying to get a fire going. We'll find them easily enough.'

'You should know better!' Jill shouted at Graham. 'If you don't set an example, how are they going to know what to do?'

Graham put his sack over his head and went back into the rain. He didn't like arguing.

It rained off and on all day. I had a look above the waterfall, but they'd have had to leave some sign, and there was nothing. It was almost impossible to get up the flooded creek; the scrub was bent beneath the weight of rain. I had to fight my way through, and soon came to a place where they couldn't possibly have got through. They couldn't even have climbed around. I turned, and Ann was right behind me.

'Not up here?'

'No.'

'Come on down,' she said. 'Jill and Graham are going to take the punt and have a look down the creek,' and we helped each other down the cliff.

CHAPTER TWENTY-SEVEN
Talking to the Baby

WE DIDN'T SAY SO BUT we were really hoping Jimmy and Derek had turned up while we'd been away. They hadn't.

We changed in front of the fire. 'Lucky we've got the chimney,' Ann said. 'These are warm and dry, and they were wet through just a while ago.

'I hope they took sacks,' she said. 'If they didn't, they'll be frozen. Here, have some fresh bread.'

It was safe and snug in the chimney. The bread was good. Outside, rain swept the clearing.

'Maybe the Japs from the gold mine came and caught them,' I said.

'They'd have waited and caught the lot of us.'

'What about those tracks in the mangroves?'

Suddenly, we were both frightened.

'I wonder who dug up the hermit?'

'Don't go imagining things, George. It couldn't be his ghost, and why would he steal them anyway?'

'We stole all his stuff.'

'That's not the same thing,' she said, but sounded less certain.

'The Wheelers wouldn't take them,' I said.

'Mrs Wheeler would take them home, if she found them. She'd put them in front of their fire, wrapped in blankets, and she'd give them hot soup. I know she would.'

'She would too, if she found them.'

'What about the graves, George? They might be there.'

'They'd have to make a shelter.'

'They did play a game there each day. Come on!'

We grabbed sacks and ran, pushing through the wet bush, but there were only the graves and their wooden slabs glistening, and the sound of rain in the leaves.

As we'd run, I'd seen a little camp, clear in my mind,

with an old tarpaulin tied to the trees, and the boys, miserable inside their sacks, waiting to be found.

'Look!'

On the baby's grave was a baked bean tin with a few blades of grass and some wild flowers from the clearing. They were fresh.

'It's a game they play,' said Ann. '*Talking to the Baby*, they call it. They talk to her, and she talks back to them. They take it in turn to be the baby.'

'What do they talk about?'

'Oh, anything, but generally it's about being unhappy. They come here and tell her when Jill's given them a telling-off, or a hiding.'

We called their names, but they weren't in the bush around the tiny clearing.

Ann's hair was wet and stuck to her forehead. 'Let's go up to the orchard,' she said.

We ran there, ran around it, calling their names, and ran back to camp. We made a stew, so there'd be something hot when they came back.

It was warm in the chimney, and our wet things steamed on us, as we chopped up potatoes, onions, and carrots, and simmered them in the camp oven. Ann skinned a stingray wing and sliced it, while I picked the bones out of some smoked fish and we added them.

It smelled good, when Jill and Graham returned, shining wet through. 'No sign?' Ann asked, but we could see, by the way they looked around the camp, they were hoping the boys were with us.

'None.' Jill was cold. They stood inside the chimney, and water made little puddles at their feet. When they were in dry clothes and sitting down, we gave them plates of stew.

'That's good,' Jill said. 'Thank goodness for the chimney! What's this? Smoked fish?'

'And the stingaree,' I said.

Jill looked funny. 'I remember Mum said once that the Bible says you mustn't eat fish without scales.'

'It says you mustn't eat pork,' said Ann, 'but we do. Anyway, you've eaten it now, so it's too late.'

Jill picked up her plate again and forgot about the Bible. We were all hungry.

'Where'd you look?' I asked.

'I went up from the creek,' said Graham, 'then turned down and came back along the edge of the river. If they'd been there, I'd have come across their tracks.'

'No sign?'

'Just some tracks we made getting oysters the other day; nothing fresh. It's funny how long tracks last in some places, even after heavy rain.'

'I looked downriver,' said Jill, 'but the tide's coming in, and I had to get back. They couldn't get across the channels anyway, not without swimming, and they're not all that good, besides, Jimmy's frightened.'

She dipped out some more stew with a mug.

'The trouble is', she said, 'they're probably hiding somewhere close by, and here we've been all over the place, getting wet through for nothing.' She sounded unconvinced.

'George went up the creek,' Ann said.

'They couldn't get up it,' I said. 'It's a torrent. There's fresh flowers on the baby's grave, so they've been there today.'

'Flowers?'

'Wild ones. Off the clearing.'

'They put them there every day,' said Ann. 'It's a game they play.'

'It's getting dark,' Graham said. 'I'm going to have another look up the orchard.'

'We looked.'

'I'll come too,' said Jill. 'We'll try yelling their names. We could have a look in the bush further up.'

Ann and I built up the fire and put more things in the stew, including the other stingaree wing.

'You don't think it's bad luck?' I said.

'If it is, it's too late now. Besides, that's just superstition.

Come on, get your sack. We'll have a look across the other side of the creek. It's the only place we haven't tried.'

Water poured over the dam, but it held well. 'I'm not walking across there,' Ann said, and we poled the dinghy to the other side.

Where the watercress patch finished, we followed the cliff. It leaned out into the bush, just as dry as the other side. Ann found a heap of bones in a dusty dry patch.

'Pigs,' I said. 'See the skull. They can't have been here, or they'd have lit a fire and stayed. They'd have been comfortable here.'

We waded through wet fern under big tea-tree. Several times, we found broken fern fronds dangling from their stems, as if somebody had marked their tracks, and I saw a few dents that might have been them, but it was impossible to say. There was some pig rooting, but there were no footprints in the freshly turned soil. We got down on our hands and knees in some places, but saw nothing.

It was quite dark, and we couldn't see very well when we turned back to where the creek should have been. We thought we were lost long before we found it, coming on it so suddenly we almost fell in. Then we had to struggle and half swim along the bank. We were exhausted when we saw the dinghy shining white in the dark. Jill and Graham were back before us, wet and silent.

Even with all our wet gear hanging around it, the chimney seemed too big for just the four of us that night.

As we went to bed, Jill said, 'Mangrove Island! The hermit's hut! We'll go there tomorrow morning.'

'How would they get there?' Graham asked. 'They didn't take the dinghy.'

'Can you think of anywhere else they might be?' said Jill.

CHAPTER TWENTY-EIGHT
Found

W E FOUND DEREK FIRST. IT had rained all night. Jill and Graham took the dinghy and rowed away in the dark. We left a stew in the camp oven and followed to the mouth of the creek. As the light came up, the punt skimmed over the mud downriver, and we saw Jill's tracks between the mangroves from the night before. We saw where she had turned back, and went on up a channel we hadn't noticed before and which petered out among mangroves. We dragged ourselves through the trees, pulling on their branches and calling. It was as if we were lost in some dark swamp where the rain never stopped.

Three channels on, Ann heard him. She was over the side of the punt, half swimming, half wading, before I saw him sitting on a tiny dry patch among the mangroves, the tide about his feet. It was his whimpers Ann heard, because he couldn't call out. He couldn't even lift his arms to her.

She had him in hers, changed him into dry clothes, and pulled a couple of dry sacks over him. She wrapped a pullover around his head, so only his face showed.

'Where's Jimmy?' she asked, cuddling Derek in the stern.

'There,' he whispered, and his head nodded wearily under the great turban of the pullover. 'Back there.' It was all he could say. He didn't seem to recognize us.

I rowed on to the next channel, one we'd searched for a campsite, and saw a set of tracks where the tide hadn't covered them. They were heading upriver and must have been Derek's.

'Where did you leave Jimmy?' I was kneeling in the bottom of the punt and begging him right in his face. He seemed to see me and turned against Ann. She bent her head.

'He says Jimmy hurt his leg last night,' she said. 'He

couldn't stand or get out of the mud, because his leg was hurting . . . in one of the channels. What's that, love?' She looked at me, and she was crying. 'Derek was trying to find his way home to get us. There!' she turned back to Derek. 'It's all right. You're safe now,' and she rocked him with her body, protecting him from the rain with her own sack.

It must have been yesterday, as Jill searched above them, and the tide came in. Derek must have tried to find his way back and got lost in the mangroves. I saw his tracks on another bank, above high water mark, and rowed up the next channel, the first one we'd followed the night we'd run away.

We were a few minutes up it, having turned in from the main river, when Ann looked, clutched Derek closer to her, trying to warm him with her body, and said, 'Over there,' and she looked down at Derek again.

Jimmy hung across the branches of a mangrove where the tide had left him last night. In another hour, it might have lifted him again, carried him up the channel, and laid him on the beach where we had spent that first night. His head hung back, his broken leg stuck out. Mud clogged his hair and clothes. His eyes and his mouth were full of mud.

I was lifting his body down, when a voice called, 'Ann! George!' Ann called back, and the voice replied. As I got Jimmy out of the mangrove, a dinghy came up the channel.

'Ann!' she called again, turned, and saw us. It was Mrs Wheeler. She ran in beside the punt, looked at Derek, jumped out and took Jimmy from my arms. 'Oh, George!' she said.

We left the punt there and got in her dinghy. As she rowed out to the river, she told us she'd seen Jill and Graham at the hermit's hut and sent them to the farm to get her husband. She'd seen us disappearing up the channel as she'd left the island and followed, calling.

She'd been searching for us ever since Mum and Aunty Iris told her we'd run away. I thought they must have been her tracks we'd seen.

Mr Wheeler met us with the launch before we were half-way across the river. They lifted Derek up and put him inside the cabin, where it was warm. Ann and I helped pass Jimmy up to them. His leg knocked the side of the cockpit with a wooden sound as they took him aboard.

Graham and Jill were there. We were all crying for Jimmy.

CHAPTER TWENTY-NINE
Going Home

I DON'T REMEMBER THE REST of that day very well. A fishing boat met us half-way across the river, and some soldiers on it took Jimmy's body aboard and set off for the Bay.

Mrs Wheeler gave us hot baths, dressed us in dry clothes, and fed us. She kept Derek wrapped in blankets in front of the fire, hot-water bottles tucked around him. We were safe and warm in her kitchen.

Then Luke Kelly's launch came in. He'd been searching the outer islands with Uncle Paul and Uncle Dugald, and they must have met the fishing boat on its way into the Bay with Jimmy. They'd picked up Mum and Aunty Iris from the bach, where they were waiting in case we came home. I think that's what must have happened. I just remember them all running in the Wheelers' door, while we were sitting around the fire. Mum was wet with rain as she hugged Jill and me and the others all at once. She couldn't stop crying, and Jill and I sat with our arms around her, but she still cried for Jimmy.

Jill said it was all her fault, but Mum just cried and said Jill had meant well. Somehow, it seemed everybody's fault Jimmy had died, and it was strange, Jill wasn't the boss any longer, just one of us again.

I can't remember much else, but going into the Bay there must have been another boat, because I could see its lights when we went past the creek mouth where the bach hid up around the corner. Ann stood by me, and we looked towards it through the darkness and rain.

Uncle Paul gave Graham a hiding, as we knew he would, but Jill told him it wasn't fair, and Ann and the rest of us cried, and Uncle Paul stopped.

Jimmy is buried in the Bay cemetery with Ann's mother and the rest of the family from ages back. We went to the old kauri church along from Aunty Iris's, then followed the coffin down to the wharf, where they lowered it on to Luke Kelly's launch and carried Jimmy across the river; they took turns carrying it up the white-stoned track above the jetty; they carried Jimmy to the grave on the cliffs, where the ground was dull red with the dead flowers of pōhutukawa.

Back at Aunty Iris's, everybody drank cups of tea and ate and talked noisily, as if they were relieved. The men went out the back and drank whisky.

We'd had to tell our story over and over again, why we'd run away and where we'd hidden, but now they left us alone and people stopped looking at us.

The Japs hadn't invaded New Zealand. We'd found out that everybody had been looking for us: the police, the Mounted Rifles, Uncle Dugald, Uncle Paul, Aunty Iris, and Mum. Dad had written at last, saying he was well, but Mum didn't want to worry him in Germany, so she hadn't told him we'd disappeared.

It was Mrs Wheeler who'd found the hermit's grave. She hadn't seen smoke for several days, and rowed up to see if he was all right. She'd got the policeman out, and he'd dug up the body. It was reburied in the Bay.

They guessed we'd buried him and taken all his things, so they searched the hills for miles up the river, especially some abandoned old farms up there. The Mounted Rifles had brought a boat from the Bay and thought they'd almost found us a couple of times. It was their camp I'd seen at the gold mine. The scrub had stopped them searching any further.

Old Mrs Cross had told Mrs Wheeler where we'd be. She remembered a family who had a small farm by a waterfall up the river. 'They all died in the flu epidemic after the Great War,' she said. 'The hermit buried them and burned down their whare.' She knew they lived up a creek above Mangrove Island, and Mrs Wheeler had kept trying to find it, but nobody else trusted Mrs Cross's memory.

A couple of days after the funeral, we were going home.

Uncle Paul was driving up to Auckland with Ann, Graham, and Derek. Uncle Dugald and Aunty Catherine were driving home in their car with us. We'd all go over the hill together. I thought it was the end of our family, that I wouldn't see Ann again.

We sat around the table at breakfast. The wireless was going, and Mum had just reminded me not to drink anything because I'd be sick going over the hill, when the news came on, and the announcer told us Singapore had been captured by the Japanese. Jill burst into tears. I'd hardly ever seen her cry before.

'We don't want to listen to that,' Aunty Iris said, switching off the wireless, but Uncle Paul and Uncle Dugald looked as if they did. And Jill sat there and cried. I looked at Mum, but she sat and didn't move. In the end, Ann and I took Jill outside. Graham and Derek joined us there, and we went and sat by the river and watched the tide till it was time to go.

Mrs Wheeler had come in to see us off, and she and Aunty Iris hugged Mum and held her for ages, and then we were leaving the Bay. When I looked back, they were still standing with their arms around each other. The tide was coming in across the pipi banks as we left the river and drove into the hills.

'That's the last of the hill,' Mum said, looking back at me in the mirror. 'It's all flat from here down to the coast.'

'Look, Uncle Paul's stopped,' said Jill, 'and Uncle Dugald's pulling up too.'

'There's somebody by the road,' said Mum. 'They just don't want to cover them in dust.'

Some children ran from a swing bridge. A couple were in the creek.

'Mum!' I yelled. 'Stop! They've got Brown! Brown!' I called out of her window.

He ran around the car and scrabbled at Mum's window, whining. Before she could open the door, he'd jumped in, scratching her and Jill and falling over the back on top of me, licking us, and giving one tremendous bark.

We got out, and the children came up from the creek and looked at us silently. Brown raced between us. Mum talked to them, and they said he'd turned up at their place before Christmas, but they hadn't got her note. She'd put it in their old letter box, one they didn't use now. We got their name and address, and Mum said she'd write and thank them properly. They waved to Brown, but he didn't look at them.

Ann got in the back with me, and we held Brown between us for the drive down the Thames coast. We had lunch on the beach at Puru. At the Kopu corner, we stopped and Ann said goodbye.

'They won't take us back to the Bay,' I whispered to her.

'It's all right,' she said. She kissed Mum and hugged Jill and me. 'We'll write to each other,' she said loudly.

Uncle Paul turned right for Auckland, and we followed Uncle Dugald straight ahead. We waved till we couldn't see each other. I hugged Brown because the family was broken up, and we didn't know if we'd ever go back to the Bay.

I sat in the back, Brown beside me in Jimmy's seat, as Mum drove up through Paeroa and Te Aroha. The grass was burnt brown by summer, and the sky was copper-coloured with smoke from the peat fires.

Brown kept whining and licking us, poking his head between the front seats and turning back to me.

'It's all right,' Mum said, and I saw in the mirror she was crying. 'He's looking for Jimmy. He'll get used to it,' and we drove on into the Waikato.

Glossary

bach   small holiday cottage
benzene   petrol
billy   pot for hanging over fire
camp oven   heavy lidded pot
chook   fowl
cicadas   shrill sounding insects
clink   gaol
conchy   conscientious objector — person who objects to fighting in war for reasons of conscience
Correspondence school   school in Wellington which teaches, by correspondence and radio, children who live in remote places
cutty grass   tall grass with sharp-sided leaves
dunny   outdoor toilet
E.P.S.   Emergency Precaution Services, a wartime organisation
flatty   flounder
fly   sheet over a tent
hurricane lantern   glass-enclosed lamp that the wind cannot blow out
infantile paralysis   polio
John Dory   New Zealand fish
kahawai   New Zealand fish
karaka   poisonous-berried tree
kauri   biggest New Zealand tree
kauri gum   hardened resin of the kauri
kerosene   paraffin
kissing crust   soft crust where loaf has touched another in baking
kit   woven flax basket
kōneke   sledge
lemon squeezer   New Zealand peaked army hat
lolly   sweet
luggage carrier   frame for suitcases on back of car
Mother Carey's chickens   stormy petrels
muster   to drive in stock
ngaio   coastal tree
nīkau   palm
noggin   short wood joints between studs
pātaka   storehouse on high legs
pāua   large shellfish
pea rifle   .22 calibre rifle
pīkau   pack made from a sugar-bag
pipi   small shellfish
pōhutukawa   spectacular red-blossomed coastal tree flowering at Christmas

ponga   tree fern
pumice   buoyant lava
razor strop   leather strap for sharpening cut-throat razor
reremai   shark
roadman   man who repairs road
saddle   crossing-place in hills
service car   motor coach, sometimes open-sided
shag   cormorant
slings of butter   wooden plank supported by a rope for loading butter on to ships
snapper   New Zealand fish
stud   upright post in building framework
sugar-bag   hessian sack in which sugar was sold
tar-seal   mixture of tar, sand, and stones for surfacing roads
tea-tree   common New Zealand shrub
twenty-two   .22 calibre rifle
undertow   back current under surface
whare   hut
wireless   radio
Zero   Japanese fighter plane

Nautical terms

ballast   weight carried low down to give boat stability
boom   horizontal spar along bottom of sail and extending its foot
bowline   the handiest knot, especially for forming loop
centreboard   vertical board raised and lowered through slot to act as keel
centrecase   box through which the centreboard is raised and lowered
cleat   to make fast a rope to a cleat
davit   crane for lifting lifeboats and dinghies
derrick   crane
gaff   spar to which head of sail is attached
gaff jaws   wooden jaws holding lower end of gaff to mast
gybe   turning the boat, when the wind is coming from behind, so the boom swings across to the other side
halyard   rope for raising and lowering sail
jib   foremost sail
mainsail   large sail behind the mast
main sheet   rope which controls and holds the mainsail against the wind

painter   rope attached to bow of dinghy, by which she is made fast

reach   sail with wind at about right-angles

reef   reduce sail

rowlock   fitting which holds oar when rowing

rudder   flat board on stern, which directs boat

scow   flat-bottomed sailing ship used for coastal trade

sheet   rope controlling and trimming sail

spar   pole holding up sail

spring tide   very high tide

stays   rigging holding up mast

stringer   long heavy timber edging the wharf.

thwarts   seats

tiller   long arm from rudder for steering

wing and wing   sailing with jib out one side, mainsail out the other

Achilles, Leander, Ajax   three smaller warships which helped defeat the German pocket-battleship *Graf Spee*

Repulse, Prince of Wales   British warships sent to help defend Singapore, and sunk by Japanese bombs

Niagara   ship sunk by mine north of Auckland

City of Benares   ship carrying British evacuee children to Canada, which was sunk